13.95

First U.S. Edition 1977
Barron's Educational Series, Inc.
113 Crossways Park Drive
Woodbury, New York 11797

Design   Michele Provinciali

Photography   Filippo Alison, Napoli   T. & R. Annan & Sons,
Department of Fine Art, University of Glasgow, Glasgow   E. O. Hoppé, Glasgow   Ziglioli & Carlotto, Milano

Translation   Bruno and Cristina Del Priore

Copyright © 1977 8693
Gruppo Editoriale Electa - Milano

ISBN 0-8120-5169-6
Library of Congress No. 77-89120

No part of this publication may be reproduced, stored in a retrieval system or transmitted in any form or by
any means, electronic, mechanical, photocopying, recording or otherwise, without the prior permission
of the publisher

Printed in Italy by Grafiche Milani, Segrate

Filippo Alison Charles Rennie Mackintosh as a Designer of Chairs

BARRON'S, Woodbury, New York

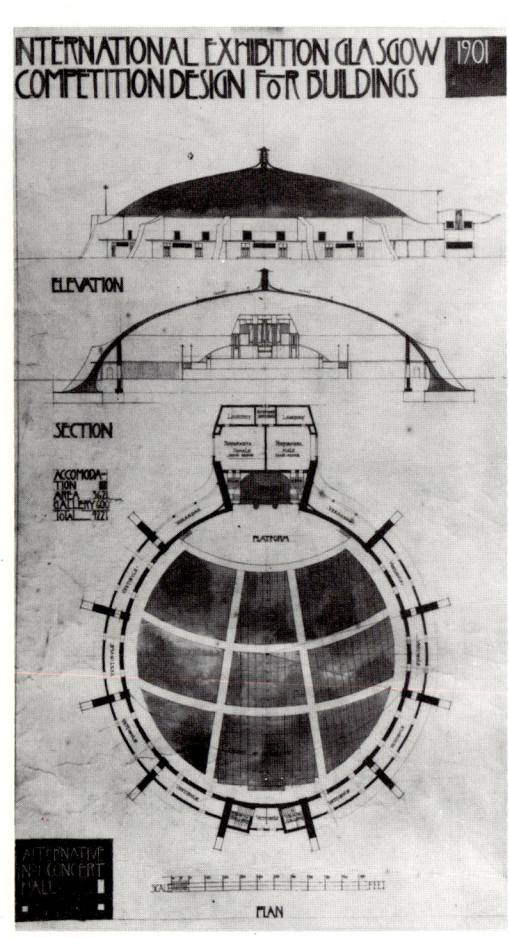

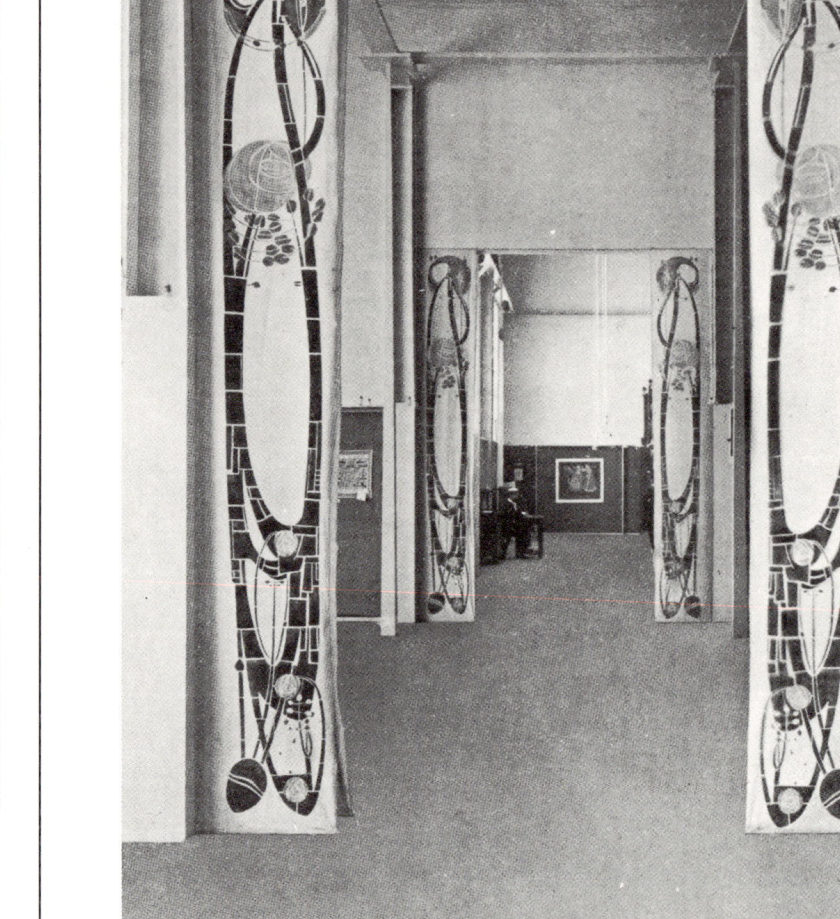

Concert hall, 1901.
4   Scottish section, Turin Exhibition, 1902.

Introduction
by Andrew McLaren Young

Mackintosh and Italy

Charles Rennie Mackintosh belonged to two worlds: a tight little northern world of Glasgow architects and their professional associations; and the larger world with no national frontiers in which the modern movement of architecture and design was born. It was so from the beginning of his career. His first independent success, the commission in 1896 for the Glasgow School of Art, came almost simultaneously with European recognition gained at exhibitions in Paris and Liège; and the completion in 1899 of the School's first stage was followed only a few months later by the enthusiastic reception given in Vienna to the furniture and objects of decorative art sent by him and his Glasgow associates to the eighth Secession exhibition. By the early 1900s there was sufficient architectural patronage in Glasgow to keep him healthily occupied; and the "Glasgow Style", of which he was the leading exponent, had become known to (and, on occasion, imitated by) architects and designers from as far apart as Central Europe and the Middle West of America.

It was, in Mackintosh's view, only proper that a Scottish architect should seek inspiration from Scottish sources. In a lecture given in 1891 on Scottish Baronial architecture he described this turreted and fortifiable style which prevailed in Scotland from the sixteenth to the early eighteenth century as the only one « we can claim as being in whole or part our own ». But, if it was right for Scots to look first to Scotland, they should avoid the kind of pastiche that at the time of Mackintosh's lecture was becoming all too common. The acceptance of a traditional idiom, Mackintosh said, should not « be strangled in its infancy by indiscriminating and unsympathetic people who copy the ancient examples without trying to make the style conform to modern requirements ». Nor, as we saw it, could architecture, if it were to be serious architecture, live in a state of national isolation.

Any understanding of Mackintosh's art must take into account its underlying — one might almost say its patriotic — Scottishness: but for Mackintosh there was no contradiction between being, at one and the same time, a Scot and a cosmopolitan. His notebooks and his sketchbooks are packed with architectural observations made not just in Scotland but in England, in France, in Portugal, in Belgium and in Italy. He was prepared to learn from wherever and whatever he was looking at: a castle in Ayrshire, a church tower in Somerset, a door latch in Norfolk, a façade in Antwerp, a brick house in Brescia, a Romanesque church in Pavia. Within a few weeks of his lecture on the very Scottish Baronial architecture of Scotland he was on a tour of Italy looking with critical eyes at famous, less famous and sometimes quite obscure buildings from Monreale in Sicily to the shores of Lake Como.

Mackintosh's Italian visit of 1891 came at a very formative period of his development. It had been made possible by a prize of £60 gained in a student competition with a design for a very unbaronial — and, to all who know his mature work, a very un-Mackintosh — looking Public Hall in what might be called the "Renaissance Manner". It is almost as though it were done with his tongue in his cheek to show his academic judges how well he could perform in the style which, as he was well aware, was regarded as appropriate for civic buildings. Mackintosh was not the kind of architectural student who saw an Italian pilgrimage as an opportunity of getting experience that could be applied to the design of Italianate public buildings. The lessons he learnt from it — and they were important ones — came rather from the study, in his own time and in his own way, of buildings which every apprentice architect had been taught to regard as central to a common European heritage. He returned to Scotland with new knowledge and heightened sensibilities, but as Scottish as he had been before he left. One of the first projects in Glasgow after his return was a competition entry for a group of tenement buildings designed in a style which exactly matched the pseudonym, "Scottish Baronial", under which it was submitted.

Mackintosh's career, as a graphic artist, as a designer of furniture and as an architect, can be said to begin with his return from Italy in the later part of 1891. During the years which followed it gathered increasing momentum until by the last year of the century the first stage of that milestone in the history of modern architecture, the Glasgow School of Art, had made its uncompromising appearance on one of the most central of Glasgow's many hills. When in 1902 he next went to Italy as the leader of the Scottish contingent in the Turin Exhibition of Contemporary Decorative Art his European reputation had already been made. Two years earlier Vienna had set the seal of approbation. « If — wrote the German critic Hermann Muthesius in 1901 — one were to go through the list of truly original artists, the creative minds of the modern movement, the name of Charles Rennie Mackintosh would certainly be included even amongst the few that one can count on the fingers of a single hand. »

Mackintosh's two visits to Italy, therefore, bracket the years that make up the first, and perhaps the major, half of his career.

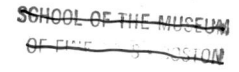

Mackintosh's Italian travels of 1891 are well recorded. There is a diary covering the whole tour. This, during the first month or so, is very full but gets a bit thinner towards the end. Shortly after his return home Mackintosh gave a lecture to the Glasgow Architectural Association in which he filled out some of the more telegraphese of the comments and added a few paragraphs about those stages of the journey completed after the diary peters out. Unfortunately the sketchbooks of the early part of the tour have been lost; but one has survived, covering all the places visited on a frequently broken itinerary from Verona to Pavia, and packed with pencil studies. Finally there are some finished watercolours and drawings made at various points of the journey: in Orvieto, Siena, Florence, Pisa, Bologna, Ravenna, Venice, Verona, Brescia, Milan, Pavia and elsewhere. (1)

The tour, somewhat unusually for that of a northern visitor, was from south to north. Mackintosh arrived in Naples by sea on Sunday 5th April; in June he was on the shores of Lake Como; he turned back to Milan on the 27th and his final sojourn was in Pavia to which he came on the 7th July.

A continuous account of the tour would extend this Introduction beyond any reasonable length. Perhaps, therefore, a few extracts — some on architecture, some personal — will give a little of the flavour of Mackintosh's experiences and attitudes during what was for him a significant stage in his process of growing-up as an architect. Wherever possible he is allowed to speak for himself.

Naples, when Mackintosh arrived there, was very wet indeed. On the 11th April he noted:

« Rose at 6.30 intending to go to Paestum but found it still raining so reluctantly postponed my departure. Spent forenoon in Museum. Cleared up about 12 o'clock; went to Certosa San Martino. One of the most interesting places in Naples. Very fine wood panelling in Conventual Hall and Chapter House. Splendid frescoes in Choir of church, splendid wooden stalls in Choir and Sacristy. The inlay work in the latter is the finest I have ever seen. »

But he was not always so appreciative:

« The Duomo being under repair and covered with scaffolding, I was unable to see much of it but what I did see I unhesitatingly pronounce as bad. »

From Naples he went on to Palermo where, after a turbulent and uncomfortable journey by sea, he arrived on the 13th April.

Bad weather was still with him:

« When I left the Consul's office it was just pouring with rain. Went as quickly as possible to the Cathedral. Went inside immediately and was most disgusted with the effect. All most miserable classic, not like the outside. Had a walk round, rather nice holy water basins. »

His great excitement in Sicily was Monreale, an excitement which he could not forgive others for not sharing:

« This fine old Monastery... gave me as much pleasure and delight as anything I saw in Italy, every bit. The exterior which is very old with its plain square tower and beautiful bronze doors; the interior, which, like the Cappella del Palazzo Reale, is covered with mosaics representing sacred history; the cloister garden — everything in fact — is fine. But there this beautiful work stands unheeded and uncared for — left to the tender mercies of two or three custodians, while the people who dwell round it, who ought to be influenced by its incomparable beauty, seem to devote all their small affections on their umbrellas — cab drivers, donkey drivers, stone breakers, policemen all carry [them]... if not for the shower then for the sunshine. »

From Palermo he returned, again very seasick, to Naples and without pause took the first train for the next, quite necessary, stage of his journey; the visit to Rome.

Although he never says so explicitly, Mackintosh seems to have been out of sympathy with Rome. He was, of course, immensely impressed with Michelangelo both as the architect of St. Peter's and as the painter of the Sistine Chapel — though of the Porta Pia he wrote, « not much to look at ». While recognising its brashness, he is quite inclined to agree with the view of the American tourist who saw the city « as a nice place, but the public buildings much out of repair ». Indeed, at times a note of Anglo-Saxon priggishness enters into his commentary:

« ...The road from the Capitol to the Coliseum, taking in the Foro Romano and the Campo Vaccino, bears a very striking appearance to some parts of the east end of Glasgow, assuming about two thirds of the population to be dead of cholera. It is as grimy, as filthy, as tumblesome, as forlorn and as unpleasantly redolent of old clothes and old women who were washerwomen once but who have long since forsworn soap... »

It was the ancient and medieval Rome, rather than the Rome of the Renaissance and later that had the greatest appeal. He regarded the church of San Paolo fuori le Mura, with its mosaics by Cavallini and its altar by Arnolfo di Cambio, as « St. Peter's not excepted, the finest in Rome ».

So, he worked his way northwards, pausing at Orvieto and reaching Siena on the 10th May. There is something of a Ruskinian note in his moralizing on the Duomo:

« The front is one of those frauds so often seen in Italy, having been considered quite independent and apart from the rest of the church, is of marble worked into innumerable arches, pinnacles, ornaments and statues, many of which are so bad and clumsy that they detract very considerably from the effect. »

But, to counter this dispraise, there is approval of the Campanile and, as a finished watercolour shows, of the Palazzo Pubblico.

In Florence, which he moved to on 19th May, nearly all his irreverence seems to have departed. The Uffizi, the Pitti, the Duomo, the Campanile and the Baptistry are all, most correctly, admired; and, in very flowery language, he was to compare the city to a « waterlily rising on the mirror of a lake ». He even tells how in a dark niche of the Duomo he, profane and Presbyterian, became « conscious... of the colour of sanctity ». It is almost as though, in surroundings so much a part of all his lessons in art history, he was overprepared for admiration.

But there were places that appealed to him more than others. The interior of Sta. Croce, for example, where he spent a day and a half sketching. And by the time he got to Pisa on 26th May the pungency of his criticism had returned:

« *Cathedral, leaning tower and Baptistry form an interesting group. Was very much disgusted with the exterior of the Cathedral. Arcades are good enough but here it is all the arcade and no design. The Baptistry is better, and the effect of the arcades on the town is very effective owing to the rows of shadow produced. But altogether the exteriors are very irritating — want some place to rest the eye. The interior is indifferently good. Best thing is the wood stalls which are very good indeed. Some nice glass.* »

The later entries in the diary become increasingly laconic. Very little is said about Pistoia and Bologna in each of which he spent a day. Even Ravenna where he stayed from the 27th to the 31st May gets less than a page. Perhaps, however, his few words were made up for by the many sketches which he tells us he made on the 29th, 30th and 31st in the Baptistry, San Vitale, Sant'Apollinare Nuovo and Sant'Apollinare in Classe. Certainly after his reactions in Monreale one would expect Mackintosh to be equally enthusiastic about the great Byzantine mosaics of Ravenna. It is sad, therefore, that the sketchbook containing the products of these three days' work have all disappeared. One watercolour of an angel and saints in Sant' Apollinare Nuovo (2) is all that remains.

From Ravenna, with a brief stop in Ferrara (where, somewhat unexpectedly, he admired Dosso Dossi), Mackintosh made for Venice. Here again, as with Florence, there is much reverence and poeticizing. But, if Mackintosh's account of Venice in the light of a setting sun is expressed in what, to post-Victorian ears, seems somewhat rhapsodic style, there is no doubt about the genuineness of his emotions. When, writing about the Ducal Palace at dusk he tells how

« *the twilight, which bats and owls love not better than I do, enlarged every portico, lengthened every colonnade, added a certain mysticism and increased the dimensions of the whole just as the imagination desired* »,

he foreshadows elements in his own architecture, elements which it is not absurd to think of as Symbolist.

In Venice it was not always the big and the Ruskin-approved that drew Mackintosh's greatest affection. On the 8th June he spent the whole day making sketches in Santa Maria dei Miracoli, a building which he describes as the « *most exquisite... the most complete little church in Venice or anywhere else* ». Increasingly in the later part of his travels he was to look beyond the standard monuments of the textbooks in which he had learnt his architectural history. He did not, of course, neglect them; but he was often to study and, indeed, to draw more from lesser buildings by obscure architects or by no known architects at all.

After brief visits to Padua (where he was impressed by the architecture, the sculpture and the religious activity of the Santo, but did not go to look at Giotto in the Scrovegni Chapel or Mantegna in the Eremitani) and Vicenza (« *better than Padua; good place to study Palladio's work* ») he arrived in Verona on 10th June. It is here that the one surviving sketchbook of his tour begins. By this time the diary had become little more than a series of brief notes; and the lecture to the Glasgow Architectural Association, which had dealt so fully with the earlier stages of the journey, had — perhaps because Mackintosh was getting worried about the time it would take to deliver it — begun to tail off. The rapid sketches — or, as at a later date Mackintosh called them, the architectural jottings — therefore fill out the skeleton of his written words. When, for example, the diary notes that the wooden stalls in San Zeno are very good, this brief comment is made clear by three pages of detailed drawings; and places, even odd architectural features, that are not even mentioned in the diary or the lecture are graphically analysed, often with measurement noted. These jottings take on a fluency which had not yet shown itself in the precise and still a little stilted studies done before he left Scot-

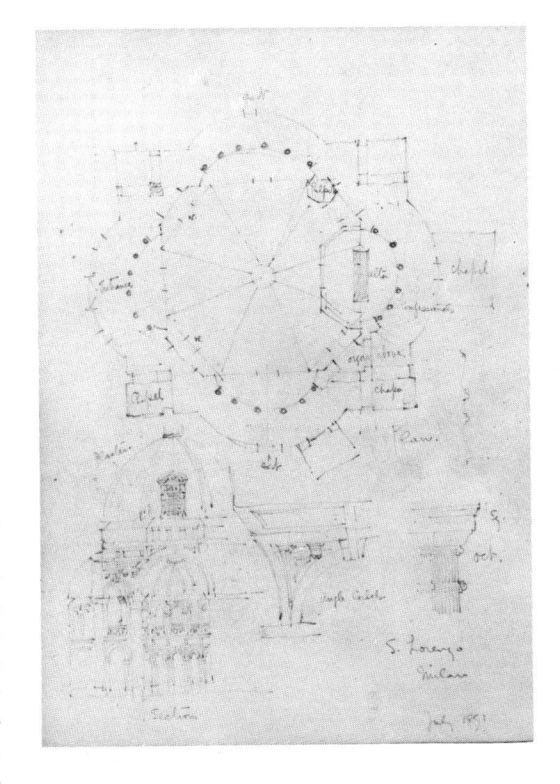

San Lorenzo, Milan.

land — or indeed, if one can judge from the few surviving examples, in the somewhat laborious water-colours of the earlier part of the tour. He was, it seems, emerging from his years of apprenticeship; and the lessons he was learning for himself in Italy were making a special contribution to the process.

So we find that in his visits to Mantua, Cremona, Brescia and Bergamo — where, apart from the Baptistry at Cremona, the Baedeker-approved architecture disappointed him — his most interesting sketches are of unpretentious and quite anonymous houses which, because of their basic form, or because of some other detail, Mackintosh saw as possessing elements from which he could learn. Here the pattern of his later architectural expeditions begins to evolve. In the 1890s, when he went to England, it was not to see the great cathedrals and country mansions but the village churches and cottages of the Cotswolds, of Devon, Somerset, Dorset, Sussex, Kent and East Anglia. These, like the modest buildings of Northern Italy, had more to teach him as an architect and as a designer than the great set pieces of architectural history.

The last great centre of architecture to be visited was Milan. He arrived there on 27th June, after a brief lakeside holiday at Cadenabbia on Lake Como and a short visit to the city of Como (« Cathedral, church of S. Fedele and the Basilica of S. Abbondio are very good »). « In Milan — he wrote — there is a lot that is worth seeing, and a great lot that isn't » — a verdict with a kind of timeless quality about it that could apply to more places than Milan. The Cathedral, in his view, was pretty evenly split into both categories:

« The old bits are rather good especially the side aisle windows. Parapet, tower all restoration, very much inferior to old work. The interior is disappointing; the effect not bad but there is a want of the grand solemnity associated with large Gothic cathedrals. »

And the windows, he wrote, were « filled with the most abominable glass ».

« There is also a beautiful fan-vaulted ceiling, which might have been mistaken for the real original had some of the plaster not fallen down, thus laying bare the deception. »

The Milanese churches that he mentions and made drawings of are, on the whole, the best-known ones: Sta. Maria delle Grazie, Sant'Ambrogio, Sant' Eustorgio and San Lorenzo. The centralized plan of the last particularly interested him. A study in his sketchbook emphasizes, perhaps exaggerates, the nearly circular form of the central area and of the ambulatory surrounding it. It is not too far-fetched to see in this drawing the germ of the idea which in 1898 went into the designing of the epoch-making concert hall which he hoped to provide for the Glasgow International Exhibition of 1901.

He enjoyed his visits to the Brera and, especially, the Poldi-Pezzoli museums. In the former there was an exhibition of contemporary Italian art of which, except for the sculpture, he did not think much. The studies in his sketchbook, though remaining informative and faithful to their subjects, take on a quality of remarkable fluidity. One of them, of a doorway in Santa Maria delle Grazie, must surely have been referred to a few years later when, behind the name of his colleague John Keppie, Mackintosh came to design the vestibule of the Glasgow Art Club.

On the 7th July Mackintosh left Milan on the final stage of his pilgrimage, a visit to Pavia. Here in the Romanesque church of San Michele, « certainly the best of its kind in Italy », he found the choir stalls covered with intarsia so fine that, for once, his sketchbook drawings are tinted with watercolour. But this « was the last place in Italy. So we returned to Milan and came home by Paris, Brussels, Antwerp and London ».

Mackintosh's Italian travels of 1891 had been paid for with the money that had come to him as the prize in an architectural competition; and his training up to that time had been pretty well the orthodox one of a Glasgow apprentice architect. Yet, as the diary and the sketchbook of his tour show, he never regarded any building as complete without its furnishing. Choir screens, carved wooden stalls, ironwork, intarsia — all he noted and described. He also visited art galleries; and in at least one watercolour made on his journey — of the Lido in Venice — architecture is so far away as to be hardly there at all. At no time in his career was he the kind of architect who, having designed the structure, could leave the details of decoration to a subordinate. Everything concerned him: the handles on the doors, the chairs and the tables, even the pictures on the walls. Indeed, in the years immediately following his return to Italy — before he was ready for independent commissions — a great part of his creative energy went into the designing of posters, metalwork, glass panels and furniture.

Although by the time of the Turin exhibition of 1902 Mackintosh's reputation as an architect had already been established in Glasgow, he was still better known abroad as the designer of portable objects that could be sent to international exhibitions. The illustrations which, from 1896 onwards, begin to appear in such journals as « The Studio », « Dekorative Kunst », « Deutsche Kunst und Dekoration », and « Ver Sacrum », are almost exclusively devoted to his work as a designer; and the influence of his style in Vienna where, as Hermann Muthesius wrote, « it found specially congenial soil », was first made through the furniture and objects sent to the eighth Secession Exhibition. Indeed the invitation to Turin came as the direct consequence of the enthusiasm which, two years earlier, the Vienna exhibition had generated.

In Vienna Mackintosh had not been alone. His friend, Herbert MacNair, and the wives of both men, the sisters Margaret and Frances Macdonald, had also been included. These young artists (to their friends in Glasgow they were known as «The Four») had in the early 1890s been the begetters of what came to be known as «The Glasgow Style». For

Turin the Glasgow Four were expanded into a national Scottish section. But, as the choice of who and what were to be included was the responsibility of Francis H. Newbery, head of the Glasgow School of Art and inspirer of the Mackintosh-MacNair-Macdonald circle, the character of the contribution remained very much the same. It was a youthful and remarkably non-pompous company: Mackintosh, at 34, was one of its oldest members.

So it came about that what, even in Glasgow, was regarded as a somewhat avant-garde coterie, took its place alongside such great national entities as Italy, Germany, Belgium, Holland and Japan. England, where the Arts-and-Crafts style of decorative art still held almost complete sway, was completely — perhaps a little aggressively — separate. Mackintosh, unanimously regarded as the Scottish "chef d'école", was in charge of the design section. In a far corner of Raimondo d'Aronco's lavishly art-nouveau pavilion — tactfully separated from England by neutral Belgians — he was provided with three empty rooms. In them he created a setting which, if a critical history of the ephemeral art of exhibition design were ever to be written, must be regarded as epoch-making. The writer in « The Studio », who was there and shared the excitement, compares it with other earlier revolutionary examples of display such as Whistler's for the Bond Street exhibitions of his etchings and pastels done in Venice.

Let « The Studio », in its own words, describe what Mackintosh did in Turin. He started with:

« Large, lofty and barn-like galleries..., entirely on the lines of the ordinary picture saloon, with windows whose light glared into every corner. [These he] ordered into a sequence of studied interdependent proportions; and the veiled daylight looks into rooms whose simple tones and harmonies afford a welcome relief to an eye tired with the glare of an Italian sun. »

Having, as it were, brought a subdued Scottish atmosphere to the Mediterranean summer, he set

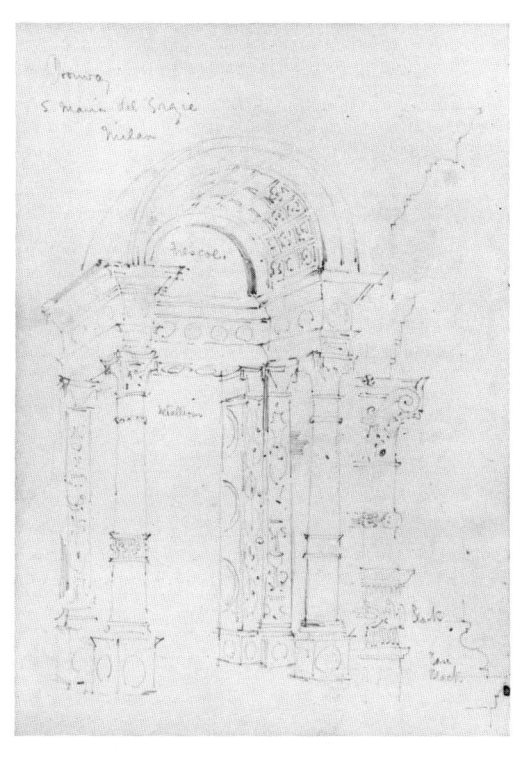

Glasgow Art Club.

Santa Maria delle Grazie, Milan.

about creating a setting for the display.

« *From the first, [he] decided that the rooms without any exhibits should be in themselves and for themselves matter for exhibition. Containing nothing, they yet should be material for study, and the exhibits should be added enrichments, and should by treatment fall into the general scheme. The spectator on entering was to be struck by the fact that here was something novel and complete in its general ensemble, and was to be insensibly led on to examine in detail the work of its parts and the matter exposed for exhibition. And as the photographs cannot give the colour scheme, here is an indication of it. The section consists of three rooms leading the one into the other, and lighted entirely from the sides by large windows, whose sills are eight feet from the ground. This gives an unbroken wall space for hanging. The first room is white, silver and rose; the second toned white and grey gold, enlivened on one wall by a frieze of pink and green; while the other and largest room is golden, purple and white. All wall spaces above the window-sill line, and all ceilings, have been whitewashed and the woodwork throughout painted white.*

A feeling of quiet repose, of coolness and of freshness, pervades the rooms; and in the work there [possesses] a reserve which recalls the temperament of the nation to which the architect belongs. A happy feature is the treatment of the electric fittings. No artificial light is to be allowed in the section, but the lamps are there. Pendant from the tops of the tall mast-like poles, or hanging from the ceiling, each on its cord of flexible wire, they give the effect of falling streams as of a white rain, while the little lamps, hanging bare and without reflectors, look like drops of water. »

The writer in « The Studio » goes on to describe Mackintosh's contribution as an exhibitor:

« *The first room on entering is occupied with the work of the architect and of his wife, Margaret Macdonald Mackintosh. Short screens, projecting into the room at right angles to the wall, indicate a division into two parts, and one of these parts has been treated as, and is called, "A Rose Boudoir." Framed into the wall at each end are two panels painted in gesso by Margaret Mackintosh. Their colour schemes are of pearly lightness, pale rose, pink, green, and blue. The subjects are decorative treatments of the figure, the forms being marked, and the surfaces led over into slight lines of coloured gesso, and broken by spots of colour. Set out on the floor are various articles of furniture, notably a black wood writing cabinet by Charles R. Mackintosh, with panels of painted gesso and of silver by Margaret Macdonald Mackintosh; chairs and a table of white wood inlaid with ivory and a chair with black and purple. A needlework panel by Margaret Macdonald Mackintosh... hangs on the long wall; and this is balanced by a silver repoussé panel by the same artist, loaned by Miss Cranston whose tea-rooms, designed by Mr. Mackintosh, are reckoned by some pilgrims to Glasgow as one of the sights of the city. Running the whole length of the boudoir is a row of silvered electric lamps, ornamented with pendants of framed pot metal, and this note is echoed elsewhere on the walls of the room by lights of a bowl-shaped form, similarly decorated. The other part of the room serves by its simple treatment as a foil to the boudoir. A few drawings well-placed, and two or three sheets from a book dealing with Mr. Mackintosh's work (one of the series on "The Masters of Interior Decoration" by Koch, of Darmstadt) comprise the exhibits in this half. The first room is the clou of the Scottish Section, and it is the epitome of work of an architect and an art-worker labouring together as copartners in the same scheme...* »

From this room the visitor passed through a wide opening to the second, devoted mainly to the work of the MacNairs and thence to the third which contained the assorted contributions of the other exhibitors, furniture by E. A. Taylor and John Ednie, needlework by Jessie Newbery, designs for interior decorative schemes by Jane Fonie and George Logan, decorative drawings for book illustrations by Jessie M. King, and metalwork, appliqué panels and book bindings by other minor figures in the group. Mackintosh reserved his boldest stroke to mark the separation of these three rooms. Flanking both openings and stretching to the full fourteen feet of each stand, attenuated female forms stencilled on linen in rose-colour, green and black. These, we are told, were not brought from Scotland but created on the spot when Mackintosh saw that the layout of the rooms called for these giant marks of punctuation. Such is the improvisation of genius. (3)

The impact made by Mackintosh in Turin set the seal on his European reputation. He was to show in other exhibitions, in Budapest, Munich, Dresden, Venice and at the invitation of Serge Diaghilev in Moscow. But the Turin display was the largest and the one over which he had the most complete control. His influence in Italy must have been felt; but, in the years which followed, his Continental contacts remained where they had begun, in Austria and southern Germany. Twice, however, in his career, and at two very decisive points, visits to Italy gave him opportunities for thought and action. The experience gained on these visits was long-lasting and profound.

(1) - The Diary and the text of the Lecture are in the Mackintosh Collection of the University of Glasgow; the surviving sketchbook belongs to the Glasgow School of Art; and the independent drawings and watercolours are in these two collections and a number of private collections.

(2) - Glasgow University, Mackintosh Collection.

(3) - « The Studio », XXVI, 1902, pp. 91-103 gives the best straightforward description of the Scottish Section of the exhibition. However, there are more and better reproduced illustrations in « Deutsche Kunst und Dekoration », XXII, 1902, pp. 575-98, in « Dekorative Kunst », V, pp. 400-15 and in « Arte Italiana (Decorativa e Industriale) », XI, 1902, pp. 62-68.

Charles Rennie Mackintosh in 1903 and in 1920.

Biographical and Critical Notes

If a few more years had been allowed to pass, a rich heritage of art treasures that bear testimony to the impassioned, inexhaustible genius of C.R. Mackintosh would have been irremediably lost. His great talent was devoted to the production of what was perhaps among the most important architecture of the years bridging the nineteenth and twentieth centuries.

Although recognition for having warned of this danger goes to Howarth (1), to whose exemplary biographical profile of the Scottish architect any future study of the subject must refer, it is Professor A. McLaren Young and his colleagues at the Department of Fine Art of Glasgow University, who deserve praise for having classified and catalogued the greater part of the most representative objects and examples produced by this artist, in particular drawings of interiors, furniture and beautiful chairs.

The survey presented here is the first attempt of its kind to present a record of that glowing period (1890-1910) which in Glasgow anticipated certain aspects of the Modern Movement in architecture so remarkably. For this survey we studied in detail original drawings and actual objects, and in an attempt to stave off the ravages of time reproduced most carefully, using a wealth of distinctive characteristics revealed by close analysis and exact measurement, as much as was possible of the vast Mackintosh production. In doing this, we tried to recover his most individual synthesis and his most sensitive connotations.

This was the only way of rediscovering the exact tone of the flowers and the leaves, so as to conserve, unchanged by time, that magic quality of his chairs, the secrets of their proportions and dimensions, in the reflective play of masses and spaces, the tensions of the curved lines in the distribution of orthogonal geometrical rhythms, the delicacy of materials, carvings and colours in the "invention" of his woven motifs.

Refined taste and a search for new architectural and design forms characterized the work of Mackintosh in the then current atmosphere of commanding Victorian eclecticism, imitation in architecture, and ugly meritless mass productions flooding the market.

His personality was certainly one of the most interesting and fecund among those who distinguished themselves in the period immediately preceeding the Modern Movement. Moreover, although one cannot describe him as a great theoretician or technical innovator, he was certainly, to use Mies van der Rohe's description, a « *purifier of architecture* ». It is in this light that the high level of formalism and the frankly figurative quality of his works should be interpreted.

In fact, anyone can verify, by thoroughly examining the sketches of interiors and furniture which he customarily prepared with great care before actually putting them into effect, that at the creative moment Mackintosh conceived the scheme in a two-dimensional form, concerning himself above all with offering an arrangement of forms complete in itself and reflecting theoretical premises which required that interior decoration should be not an empty glitter but a new medium for new ideas. This was no small aim, considering that this assumption, to which Mackintosh remained absolutely faithful, virtually amounts to a conscious break with the tradition and recurrent culture of his day, which still maintained that architecture was the art of decorating constructions.

Mackintosh the designer revealed himself in 1894 when he was about 26 years old. From that period on, he was truly engaged in designing furniture and in his free time carried out various craft and decorative commissions in a little studio rented the following year.

Amongst the first of his works worth mentioning were several pieces intended as wardrobes for the general market, ordered by the firm of Guthrie and Wells of Glasgow.

These were simple and relatively austere designs whose rigid rectangularity was relieved only by a long, sweeping, carefully placed yet almost casual curve, and by accessories like the medieval-style hinges. Mackintosh avoided the use of varnish and used only green and dark brown stain. The result was really quite similar to the simpler products of the Arts and Crafts School. The essential difference is in Mackintosh's tendency to build structural elements which often seem so subtly different from the familiar vernacular robustness. Such was the new trend of designers who found inspiration in Japanese images and paintings, whose main characteristic is an absolute absence of any sign of depth, deliberately aimed to accentuate the decorative effect of the work through a marked two-dimensional quality.

Nevertheless the ideological assumptions of Ruskin, Morris, Lethaby and Voysey can be traced in the formation of a sensibility which imposed a radically new manner of conceiving the sub-division of space and, consequently, a different decoration of the walls, in order to integrate them into the living body of their environment.

This sensitivity was a particular gift and characteristic of Mackintosh's; he included the walls in the overall context of the design, regarding them as the Archimedean node of spatial articulation, while leaving the furniture and furnishings to sustain the arrangement of the interior as a whole. Of the furniture, the chair (particularly when high backed) perceived in its iconographic and almost fetishistic quality, was the object which he felt best delineated space.

In this respect Mackintosh's work was the first manifestation of the practical décor which his predecessors had only theorized about for half a century without ever verifying the value of their theories. There can be no question but that the appellation « pioneer of modern art » is given to him for this reason also.

Certainly the foundations of the Modern Movement had not yet acquired that full canonical formulation which came after Mackintosh:

« ... to rid interior decoration of all pseudo-decorative superfluity, to turn straight to the clarity and representativeness of the idea, to avoid any impression of casual assortment, to create environments and not to overload interiors with furniture and objects, so that in the harmony of the environment man can recognize the natural place of his civil existence... » (2). These are principles which imply a deeper knowledge of the social problems connected with modern production techniques, and were still to come, however they may be interpreted, at the time when Mackintosh designed the interior of his own flat in Mains Street, Glasgow, Hous' Hill in Glasgow, Hill House in Helensburgh and Windyhill in Kilmacolm.

This is why limiting the evaluation of that architecture to simple considerations of an aesthetic nature is to deform the meaning of that new form of composition which Mackintosh, not without awareness, proposed in the examples of his interiors; although some people, such as Vittorio Pica, went further in referring to the interior arranged by Mackintosh himself on the occasion of the 1902 Turin Exhibition.

According to Vittorio Pica the visitor had to: *« ... agree that the set "Rose-Boudoir" shows such an exquisitely harmonious accord of soft hues and graceful lines, that one's eye experiences a rare aesthetic delight, and in contemplation the prettiest poetic visions are aroused in the mind. »* (3)

Nor was Mackintosh made any better known to a wider public by having attributed to him solutions suitable only for an élite: *« ... thus [they] come to create an exceptional decorative art of gentle, womanly grace and subtle, evocative efficacy, that in its frail but convenient abnormality surely is assuredly not very suited to mortals... »* (4), because Mackintosh had never betrayed his purpose, arrived at through the programmes of the Guild and the Arts and Crafts movement, which was not to limit the audience for his works to a select few. His many creations for everyday life — flower vases, ornaments, cutlery — confirm this.

In general one can affirm that, in the formative evolution of an artist, there is always an experience which, more than any other, contributes to the development of his personality, perfecting or sometimes indeed forming, these characteristics which will, for his whole working life, be recognized as the distinctive patrimony of the artist himself. In Mackintosh's case there is little doubt that the cultural matrix can be traced in terms of academic ideology and indigenous traditions. The fundamental harmonic scheme, the underlying tensions of the structure of both objects and buildings, are typically Scottish and are recognizable in his whole work. Notwithstanding this, the spirit which shaped him had the dimension of one who had truly absorbed the architectonic culture of the Mediterranean world, especially that of the Italian Renaissance.

He felt the fascination of Renaissance solutions, particularly in the rigorous order and openness of its figurative essence. Once Mackintosh reached Italy and was confronted with Romanesque façades, fifteenth century towers and churches, his mind was enriched through a detailed survey of decoration and distribution of spaces of all Italian architecture, in short, and was clearly influenced by this experience.

At that time in middle class British homes there was still a firm tradition of sending children to Italy on a cultural "tour", and this was indeed a fundamental stage in the life of anyone aspiring to distinction in that society. For Mackintosh, therefore, a journey of this kind signified the crowning of his hopes, and his opportunity came from the Xth Thomson competition, which he entered with a design for a public hall to seat one thousand people, presented in Gothic Style as in the terms of the competition, but in a Greek Renaissance key.

In February, 1891 Mackintosh left Glasgow for his continental tour. His diary, a notebook now kept at the University Art Collection, Glasgow, notes his arrival at Naples on the 5th April, and subsequently his visit to Palermo, Rome, Orvieto, Siena, Florence, Pisa, Pistoia, Bologna, Ravenna, Venice, Bergamo, Como, Milan and Pavia, before the 7th of July.

Although the notes on his tour were scanty and rather frivolous (observations on Partenopean clamour and descriptions of occasional encounters, with no mention at all of many of his visits to cities in Northern Italy, for example), in contrast the diary abounds in interesting architectural sketches and reliefs. He shows a vivacious predilection for inventiveness and in consequence a lively sympathy for those Masters, starting with Michelangelo, who had exercised originality rather than academic tradition, however noble and exquisite the latter may have been. An intelligent and critical observer, he took note of all the more outstanding accomplishments of the great Italian architects and recorded the most significant as though they might help him to clear up certain nebulous problem areas of his own. Only by taking this into account can one interpret the purpose of that heterogeneous harvest of sketches which is his diary. Here one finds elevations, sections and plans of the most conspicuous examples of Italian architecture without any reference to their respective historical periods. He also made sketches of details, sections of pillars, profiles of head friezes, and mouldings, making a collection which some experts take to indicate eclectic taste and interests. In reality, if he had made an academic and systematic study of the history of Italian art, little would have remained his, even as part of his deep creative source of inspiration. What was essential for him was to register what may be defined as the most representative and formative features of Italian architecture. Thus he was able to deposit in his artistic subconscious the formal essence of classical Italian architecture to be added to his already acquired experience. This tempered his northern qualities and eventually leavened the cultural matrix from

Rose Boudoir, Turin Exhibition, 1902.

16 *The Castle, Brescia.*   *Santa Maria Maggiore, Bergamo.*

which the best part of his work was derived.

It is really this classical component with its precious combination of cultural elements which explains Mackintosh's success on the continent: this was demonstrated in Vienna and in Turin and is still demonstrated today by the careful re-appraisal of the significance of his works.

On his return from Italy Mackintosh again worked as an assistant in the firm of Honeyman and Keppie, with which he was associated from 1889, while he attended, with increasing involvement and profit, evening classes at the Glasgow School of Art, where he had been a student since starting as an apprentice in the office of the architect John Hutchison in 1884.

One must remember that until the end of the nineteenth century public institutions with courses in architecture did not exist in Scotland. The training of young architects took place in the offices of already established architects, with a didactic procedure very similar to the practice of the great masters of the fourteenth and fifteenth centuries. Official recognition of an architect, therefore, did not derive from the completion of a diploma course but from works which were presented to the public and from the judgements, above all in competitions, which were given by the experts of the day.

Having won that first prize of sixty pounds in the Thomson competition which permitted him to undertake his Italian journey, and been awarded first prize at the annual exhibition of the students of the School of Art, in which he participated with a selection of sketches jotted during his Italian itinerary, Mackintosh distinguished himself and became known as the most promising student among those registered in the Glasgow School of Art courses. This sanctioned and extended the reputation of the artist throughout the area, the School being the most prestigious centre of cultural interests, due above all to the wisdom and diligence of its director Francis Newbery, who later became the friend and protector of C. R. Mackintosh.

On this theme it is worth mentioning the incisive portrait which Macleod (5) drew of the artist: « ... *he had, however, made a small but real student reputation; he was undoubtedly a "promising young man". He was employed in a firm which appreciated his abilities, and in which his responsibilities were widening. He was pleasant, gregarious, and articulate. He was passionately involved with his craft, and if obdurate and self-willed, his energy, idealism, and marked abilities made these qualities acceptable to those around him...* »

Apart from his participation in annual competitions for the Soane Medallion, re-commencement of evening studies in the Glasgow School of Art, and apprenticeship with Honeyman and Keppie, there is little evidence of Mackintosh's activity during the two years following his return from the Continent; however, this remains perhaps the most pregnant period in the formation of the artist. In the drawings for these competitions, in the projects planned for Honeyman and Keppie, one can recognize those original signs which later constituted the most valid part of Mackintosh's morphological and semantic language.

Certainly his productions could not yet be organically defined, still less unified, nor was that quality which was shortly to mark his work apparent at this time. One can presume, however, that just in this period Mackintosh's extremely refined sensibility and his psychic restlessness were utterly involved in seizing every communication, no matter how faint, which in any way might announce some fresh innovation in the field of art.

This may also be inferred from Mackintosh's early involvement with new artistic trends, as the magazine « The Studio » (6) announced in Glasgow in the Autumn of 1893. His first Art Nouveau work was in fact to be seen in the same year in a diploma design for the Glasgow School of Art Club.

In the same period, Mackintosh met the Macdonald sisters, Margaret, whom he was later to marry, and Frances. The two sisters, both pupils of the Art School, enjoyed the protection and esteem of Francis Newbery, head of the School of Art and himself an excellent artist. With these two talented girls, and with Herbert MacNair, Mackintosh began a long-lasting, binding relationship in the group called "The Four", producing that style which has become known as the "Spook School".

The first works of the group (7), using mostly graphic methods which resemble William Blake's, and later influenced by the Pre-Raphaelite Brotherhood, presented a series of justifications with a content of almost Ossianic derivation. Muthesius speaks of this when he writes about the interiors exhibited in the Scottish section of the Turin Exhibition:

« ... *The human figure there seems to be only a creative pretext; by its representation they [the artists] aim at nothing but a soothing lull of lines; it is stretched in length or twisted in all directions according to needs, but it always remains exclusively decorative. It is stylized just as the English art has stylized the plant; it is constructed and warped in posture of ornament to match with such and such a leading line. In this way we get the last consequences of the decorative line whose source must be traced in England. Blake had already been enraptured by it a hundred years earlier and Rossetti promoted it to the whole world. From Rossetti and the Pre-Raphaelites the way goes straight on to the Dutch Toorop as well as to the Artists from Glasgow...* » (8)

At the end of the century Mackintosh's fame had grown and was consolidated mainly by the interior design of the Tearooms commissioned by a certain Miss Cranston.

For such a singular institution as that of the Tearoom there existed no precedents, and this development may be attributed to the business acumen of Miss Cranston, probably derived from a desire to satisfy her refined need for good taste. These needs found Mackintosh's talents indispensable, and he interpreted them correctly, conducting the operation, designing interiors where shop assistants and wives of industrialists could gather together for afternoon encounters in a fanciful, clean atmosphere which could offer them the illusion of having escaped from the daily grind of a grimly impenetrable city.

Mackintosh designed everything for these rooms — crockery, cutlery, vases, materials, chairs, carpets, glass, panels worked in iron, and murals, all planned and actuated organically without any recourse to the fashion of the moment, with a global expression of space which is without precedent in the history of architecture unless you go back as far as Michelangelo's Laurentian Library.

It is worth while considering the importance which G. C. Argan ascribes to this new approach in architecture:

« *Between the interior and outer spaces comes about a continuity of style. This is also supported by new techniques that over-*

come the traditional static ratio, allowing the empty to prevail over the mass. From the minimum scale of the interior furnishings we pass to the maximum scale of the town décors. In this sense the library of the Glasgow School of Art is typical; the architectural space is determined beginning from the inside, the objects and furniture, and then spreads into the complex and plastic structures of the shelves, which in their material and constructive articulation recall the techniques of furniture rather than those of architecture... » (9)

It is to be noted, as need hardly be suggested, that the stylistic continuity described by the Italian critic in the example of the School of Art evolved in Mackintosh from a stable and clear vision of total organization of the environment. This was at the base of his later compositions, and perhaps even constitutes their fundamental value.

There is much evidence of this in his work. Suffice it to consider the tradesman's entrance to the garden of Hill House, Helensburgh (1902). Here the composition does not exhaust its meaning in itself, but has the capacity, despite certain facile tricks, of extending the internal space beyond the boundary. This capacity is such that the external observer does not become aware of any break in the environmental unity. Even whilst outside the dwelling, he has the vivid impression of being in it.

The austere symbols of Scottish baronial architecture, its spirit, the Gothic element of Northern Medievalism, are the cultural sub-structure into which Mackintosh later inserted the rampant floral decorative element of Art Nouveau.

Certainly such a combination is made even more complex by the individual elements which run through it and which can be isolated as such. In Mackintosh's work, at least as far as the design of furniture is concerned, the Gothic component can be reduced to its essential dynamic essence.

In other words, the traditional Celtic pictorial graphics are reduced to an esoteric symbol with a stimulating rôle quite antagonistic to complacency. The volumes and the masses of baronial buildings and traditional Nordic furniture are purified to a geometrical perfection in primary solid shapes. The Art Nouveau component, whose decorative function in the most extreme examples of Beardsley and Morris is almost entirely two-dimensional, is enriched by Mackintosh with a perspective element which he even uses to further emphasize the two-dimensional. This is particularly true for objects rather than for other works such as water-colours. The structure of a chair, in fact, can always be reduced to a harmonious orthogonal scheme, to the rythmic modulation of which the perspective dimension converges in its tone-colour function. In studying and identifying objects we have always made use of this theoretical scheme and it can always be traced back to that austere monastic echo of the medieval Scottish form, tempered, however, by Mackintosh's skill.

According to this analysis, the complex system of formal and functional values, even when elaborated at different levels depending on the diverse destination of the projected work, will always result in a disciplined unity bearing the mark of the elegance of the architect, and will reach a conclusion in that extreme simplicity of figuration which remains one of Mackintosh's most precious characteristics.

« ... In these works a stylistic dualism seems to exist: Mackintosh moved with ease and confidence from the then most delicate rhythm, which hovers in a world of olive-green and ivory-white harmonies, to the most ponderous cubes, which constitute integral elements in a system of rectilinear surfaces of dark green and black. » (10)

Another revolutionary component in Mackintosh's artistic physiognomy, a component indeed present in all his work, is the assumption of the decorative rôle of the structure. If one considers that at that time the idea of the ornamental function of structure was still a futuristic concept, one is led to the conclusion that the work of this master presents itself as something new in the history of interior design.

Thus the observations of Pevsner seem most congruous, for it was he who saw the origin of the ornamental quality of Mackintosh's works within the contrast of heterogeneous composite elements.

« What characterizes all Mackintosh furniture can be said to be a successful synthesis of the contrasting criteria of England and the continent. » (11)

And then again:

« These sophisticated, precious colours harmonized to perfection with the sophistication of his slender uprights and shallow curves. » (12)

One understands, therefore, how anyone who wished to attribute prevalence to one or other only of the many aspects of Mackintosh's works, would finish by altering his artistic physiognomy. Very rightly, the English scholar emphasizes again:

« ... Here was the wilfulness and irregularity of Art Nouveau handled with an exquisite finesse previously unknown. But here was also a sense of slender, erect verticals and smooth, unbroken surfaces which might well serve as a weapon to defeat Art Nouveau. » (13)

Cabbages in an Orchard, 1894.

20

Hill House, Helensburgh, tradesmen's entrance from the road; tower corner; the window of the bedroom; service door from the garden; tower corner.

Thus Pevsner outlines how Mackintosh in fact, rather than submitting to the influence of the New Style, mastered it. Bending it to his will, he utilized it in the most fitting way for his own design purposes.

« Mackintosh alone, we repeat, could be a witness for the defence and for the prosecution of both Art Nouveau and anti-Art Nouveau. » (14)

These ten years between 1897 and 1907 were Mackintosh's fullest both in terms of work and fame. It is no exaggeration to claim that in fact after the Vienna Exhibition (1900) and the Turin Exhibition (1902) the Scotsman was the best known living architect in Europe.

In Austria the « Vereinigung bildender Künstler Osterreichs », known after Hoffmann joined them as the Viennese Secession (July 1897), found a natural affinity with the Scottish approach which was widely proselytized in Europe on the wave of comments from critics which followed the publication of « The Studio ». (15)

On the 20th of April, 1900, in an atmosphere of fervid preparation for the 8th Exhibition of the Secession, Hoffmann, the idol of the younger generation of Viennese architects and organizer and designer of the Exhibition, invited Felician Freiherr von Myrbach, at that time director of the Department of Graphic Arts and subsequently principal of the same Kunstgewerbeschule, to go to the Guild of Handicraft at Essex House during his imminent visit to England.

« That is where C. R. Ashbee works... It would be worthwhile to show the real British design in Vienna for once. It would be a powerful blow to the Museum. Here we have hitherto seen only old things or export merchandise. » (16)

He was urged by his interest in ranging modern production against the traditional objects which many British artists had for several years been showing at the various expositions of the Künstlerhaus. In fact, J. E. Boehm exhibited in 1882, Herkomer in 1888, and then successively J. R. Reid in 1892, H. W. B. Davis, W. W. Ouless, E. A. Abbey, E. O. Ford and A. Hacker. W. Crane, W. Morris and J. R. Reid participated in the Jubilee Exhibition in 1898 set up in the Musikverein room. Crane also had a one-man show from the 31st December 1900 to the 10th February 1901, in the Museum für Kunst und Industrie. Nor were Scottish artists lacking, in the 7th Secessionist Exhibition from March to May 1899, where Macaulay Stevenson, Thomas Grosvenor, Edward Hornel, David Gauld and Joseph Crawhall were all represented.

In Britain in the meantime, "The Four" had taken up a position of open dissent against the artist-artisan disciplines of the Morris school of thought. Morris himself had, in a paper published in 1893 for the Society of Arts and Crafts Exhibition, stated that of the contemporary interpretations of art only two were serious, namely his own and that of his followers, and that of the "Aesthetes".

This climate, which conceded nothing other than that little liberty related to the function, favoured the dismal failure of Mackintosh's and his group's works which were presented at the 1896 exhibition held by the Arts and Crafts Society. This failure brought about the exclusion of "The Four" from the exhibition the following year.

The works — a number of posters, some decorative panels in glass and metal by the Macdonald sisters, and a bench by Mackintosh himself — were considered the antithesis of the other movements in the field of the decorative arts in Britain. Nonetheless, the view reported in « The Studio » was on that occasion more than favourable:

« The Misses Macdonald show so much novelty and so much real sense of fine decoration in their works that a tendency to eccentricity may be easily pardoned. But this same tendency constitutes a very real danger: and those who are most eager in defending the posters and various subjects from their hand, should also be quite candid in owning that "The Spook School" is a nickname not wholly unmerited. » (17)

Obviously Mackintosh's pieces with their symbolic lines which appeared to flow together in a magic ritual system, created no less of an upsurge of indignation. However, the critic concluded:

« Probably nothing in the gallery has provoked more decided censure than those various exhibits; and that fact alone should cause a thoughtful observer of art to pause before he joins the opponents. If the said artists do not come very prominently forward as leaders of a school of design particularly their own, we shall be much mistaken. » (18)

This kind of judgement and the important article published in « The Studio » the next year, must have influenced Hoffmann in particular, who, in the 8th Exhibition of the Secessionists, reserved the «Ver Sacrum» room for thirty-three works of the Mackintosh-MacNair-Macdonald group.

When and how Mackintosh came to Vienna has not been exactly established. It is presumed that he was invited on behalf of Hoffmann by the banker Wärndorfer. According to what Ludwig Hevesi wrote in 1905, in all probability this "Kunstfreund", also with contributions from other enthusiastic patrons, offered Mackintosh and Margaret, who had recently become his wife, six weeks' residence in Vienna. The records note significant examples of enthusiasm both on the part of the public and amongst the critics for the couple and for their work. Hevesi, the most influential art critic in Vienna at the time, wrote in one of his three articles on the exhibition:

« *A white room in what we call the "Brettlstil", with scattered white squares of decoration and smoky water-colours of fairytale scenes, black stiff-necked furniture, strangely embroidered strips of frieze, copper repoussé articles with the character of crushed crinkled sheet metal; coloured glass in similar designs; in the décor a predilection for spectral and grotesque human forms, whose excessive thinness gradually leads into threadlike linear curves. The element of whimsical caprice that we in Vienna call "Gschnas", is strongly in evidence so that the room takes on the character of a private sanctum set aside for certain exceptional moods. But behind the foolery there is a remarkable talent; the artistic specificity of the whole is never lost.* » (19)

The simplicity of the Glasgow School had therefore struck Viennese taste. The works of Ashbee (1863-1942), founder of the Guild and School of Handicraft in 1888, did not win so much admiration. Hevesi had this to say on the subject of the artist:

« *He himself is a rough and ready workshop man, even in his decorative objects, which might be taken for domestic folk art... The furniture displayed here leaves the Viennese (with a few exceptions) fairly cool. The workmanship, when compared with that of our own present-day craftsmen, spurned though they are by the Secession, is rather primitive.* » (20)

The critics were almost unanimously in favour of Mackintosh. There is another famous opinion, given this time by Richard Muther, also on the occasion of the 1900 exhibition:

« *Go through the rooms of an exhibition, whether in Vienna, London, Paris or anywhere else, and you will be aware of a great degree of unity of tone. You stand perhaps in the room of Mr. and Mrs. Mackintosh, you see thin, tall candles, chairs and cupboards thrust upwards in pure verticals, pictures with slender elliptical figures whose outlines are governed by the linear play of a unifying thread. You have seen Mrs. Mackintosh herself, standing in the room like a Gothic pillar. Her hat was the capitol, the perpendicular folds of her long mantle provided the fluting. Just imagine Mrs. Mackintosh in a blouse with wide, bulky sleeves, in a jacket which exaggerates the hips; imagine the pictures on the walls replaced by others by Makart, the rectilinear flower vase by the fat-bellied flower basket, the delicate vertical lines of the light fitments by an overhanging Baroque chandelier; and it will feel like a slap in the face. The stylistic unity of the room has become manifest to you.* » (21)

The story of Mackintosh's participation in the Vienna exhibition is condensed in these extracts. But besides the official recognition Vienna offered a golden opportunity to the Scot: the acquaintance of Hoffmann with whom, even though at different levels, Mackintosh had artistic ideals in common.

This comparison, however, despite their mutual knowledge of Voysey and Scott in particular, finds a common link at best on the aesthetic plane. Mackintosh was by far the more outstanding, due to the excellence of his formalistic contribution and because of certain distinctive tones of social sensibility. However, there are also the characteristics which most significantly separate Mackintosh from the main line of Art Nouveau, as this mode was evolved through Morris, the Domestic Revival and the Kelmscott Press, and then through Mackmurdo and Beardsley.

Mackintosh's presence in Vienna left another effective mark; Behrens took for himself that model of rectilinear functionalism which was a particular characteristic of the Scot. Thus the style of "The Four" was enlarged and reflected in Austria and Germany; a style which in its complex system of verticalism, in its superficial planes and elementary solids, offers its most typical characteristics. The work of "The Four" aroused equal interest at the 1902 Turin Exhibition, about which there are abundant comments, not all of them apologetic.

After Turin, where Mackintosh had, as was usual for him, personally arranged each piece of furniture and each item in the "Rose Boudoir" setting, his name became known all over Europe. His designs were exhibited in Venice, Munich, Budapest and Dresden. The invitation to exhibit in Vienna was repeated in 1905.

In his very well-known biography, Howarth quotes certain sources of information from which it would seem that besides an exhibition in Berlin before 1905, the Parisians were to have arranged an exhibition in 1914 to present « The Splendour of Mackintosh » but this was never realized because of the outbreak of the Great War.

Finally, one reads in an essay by Chapman Huston reported in « Artwork »:

« *The Grand Duke Serge of Russia — he writes — visited the Turin exhibition and was so enamoured of the work of the Mackintoshes that he became one of their most*

24 *Wall decoration, Buchanan Street Tearooms, 1897.*

ardent admirers and invited them to give an exhibition in Moscow under Imperial patronage. This they did in 1913. Their work was received with acclamation by the Russian artists and public; it secured an instantaneous success. Everything was sold except the carpet, designed by Mackintosh, which had been specially made for the floor of the exhibition room. » (22)

Whilst Mackintosh's prestige grew abroad, and the works of "The Four" were widely publicized by Koch and Muthesius, almost all the efforts of the Scot to actuate that new distribution and organization of space which would have smoothed the path of the Modern Movement were almost completely disregarded.

The hostility of English circles, a hostility which we must remember had been shown towards Mackintosh since the 1896 London Arts and Crafts Exhibition, has some complex and in some ways obscure aspects. One of the most widely held opinions attributes such hostility to the fact that the English were little taken with Art Nouveau, and that thus Mackintosh could expect but little acceptance. Those who credit this opinion do not take into account the fact that Mackintosh's work passes beyond Art Nouveau, and that, indeed, in certain mature examples of his work and in the climax of his isolation, the Scot positively anticipates the future, albeit in schemes which were at one with his traditional architecture. Such is the case with the wallpaper in the house at 78, Derngate, Northampton.

Concerning the unjust indifference the English reserved for his work, M. Amaya, in his valuable guide to Art Nouveau, expresses himself thus:

« *That Mackintosh should have been an*

inspiration on the Continent in the important transition from curvilinear Art Nouveau to rectilinear Art Nouveau, while he was virtually ignored in England, is one of the many ironies of his mercurial career as an architect, which ended in total eclipse. Strangely, it may have been because he was accepted so completely in Germany and Austria that he was ignored at home during the anti-German campaign of the first world war. A nation at war might easily have forgotten that Mackintosh and the Scottish School had inspired the "Huns". The Germans for their part, with their love of methodical arrangement, mathematical precision, tidy living and orderliness, found in Mackintosh what they could not find in Van de Velde or in the French.

In Mackintosh's work, one can discern today one of the major elements of Art Nouveau. For it was more than just a momentary stop-gap phase in decorative design, wallowing in its own whip-lash motifs; rather it was a genuine search for the new which resulted not only in a new style of curvilinear, organic invention, but in a whole new vocabulary of rectilinear functional form, which made possible the language of the Bauhaus and contemporary design. » (23)

These and other motivations, such as a possible physical decline of the artist, do not fully explain, and certainly do not justify, the scant consideration in which men of his time, particularly his fellow countrymen, held him.

The consequences of such unjust and inexplicable hostility would have lasted a long time, indeed until quite recently. Except in his own region of origin, his name and his works were completely ignored.

One must deduce indeed, that the misunderstanding continues to this day, if one accepts the following interpretation of a normally attentive critic:

« *He was not, therefore, a total phenomenon, an isolated genius without ancestry or progeny. He was rather a last and remote efflorescence of a vital British tradition which reached back to Pugin. He could not perhaps have existed apart from his isolation, but he could not in the end have any succession because of it. With his pursuit of the "modern", his love of the old, and his obsessive individuality, he was one of the last and one of the greatest of the Victorians.* » (24)

Here we feel obliged to make an unusual digression and pause briefly to consider the above quotation.

If one wishes to consider as the last of the Victorians the man who expressed the most exquisite essence of the latter half of the nineteenth century and consigned its lasting imprint to the future to flower, then we accept such a definition as ours, convinced as we are of Mackintosh's unsurpassed rôle.

But, if this comment has a less all-embracing connotation, and if its meaning is limited (and we fear this is the intention of the critic), we cannot but reject it as the result of a hasty judgement, arising in part from that, alas, all too common misunderstanding, which is wont to make rigid classification of a historical cultural period for the sake of convenience.

Mackintosh's volatile and cantankerous nature, the intolerance of his companions in the studio where he worked, especially that of Keppie, induced Mackintosh to leave Glasgow in 1913 and to move to the Suffolk coast where he spent a year or two painting and resting.

In 1915 he moved to Chelsea. Here Mackintosh had, besides the house we have

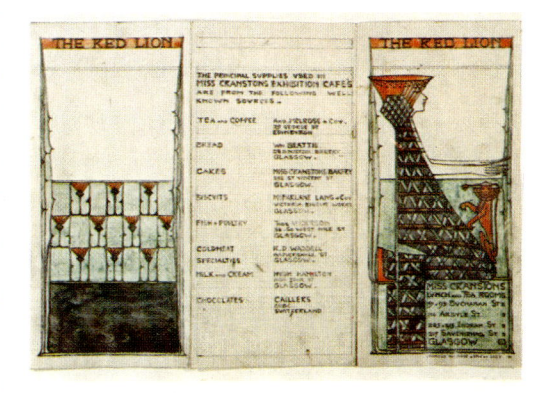

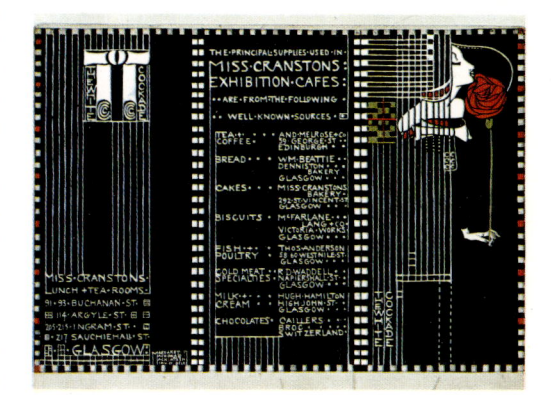

Frances Macdonald: design for menu card for Exhibition Café "The Red Lyon".

Margaret Macdonald: design for menu card for Exhibition Café "The White Cockade".

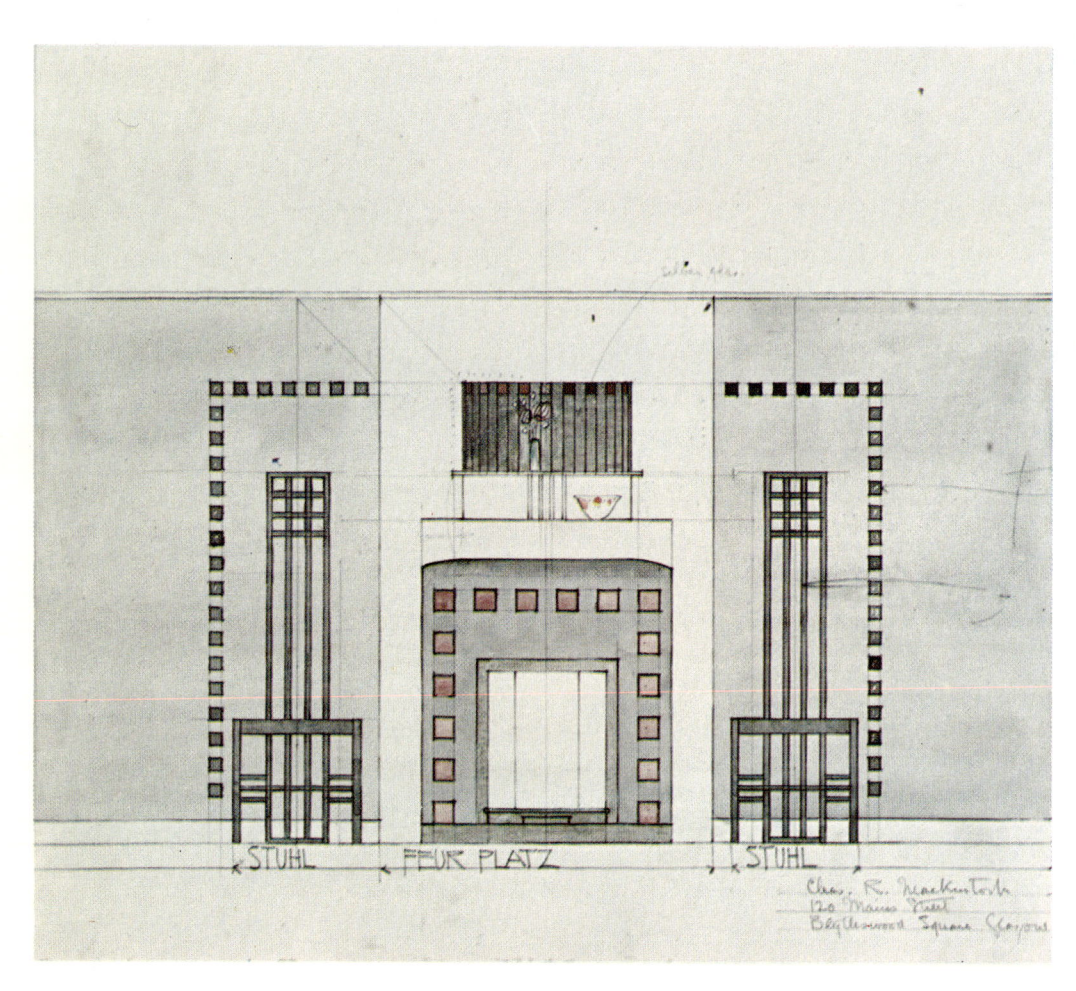

mentioned, commission for houses and studios for three artist friends; houses which, alas, were never constructed. Finally in 1920, on a commission from Margaret Morris, he designed a theatre which also remained unrealized. By then, tired and disappointed, Mackintosh decided to retire farther south to the bright skies of the French Mediterranean coast, at Port Vendres. In this period, having somewhat got the better of his drinking vice, Mackintosh painted about forty superb water-colours of landscapes, still-lives, flowers and plants.

In 1927 he got cancer of the tongue, and on the 10th of December of the following year he died.

26 *Design for fireplace for an Austrian or German client, 1900-1903.*

(1) - Thomas Howarth, « Charles Rennie Mackintosh and The Modern Movement », Routledge and Kegan Paul Limited, Glasgow University Press, 1952.

(2) - Rossana Bossaglia, « Il mobile liberty », De Agostini, Milano 1968, page 10.

(3) - Vittorio Pica, « L'Arte Decorativa all'Esposizione di Torino 1902», Istituto Edizioni d'Arti Grafiche, Bergamo 1903, page 212.

(4) - V. Pica, op. cit., page 26. Pica can be excused for such a judgement. Probably he lacked the necessary information for assigning a correct historical place to Mackintosh. But it is inconceivable that a contemporary historian of the Art Nouveau movement could express the same opinion today.

(5) - Robert Macleod, « Charles Rennie Mackintosh », Fletcher and Son Limited, Norwich 1938, page 30.

(6) - In the September issue « The Studio » presented « The Three Brides » by Toorop, a work which was immediately to influence a whole generation of artists.

(7) - « Girl in the East Wind », 1893, by Frances Macdonald; « 5th November », 1894, by Margaret Macdonald; « A Pond », 1894, by Frances Macdonald; and by Mackintosh himself after the diploma, « Spring » of 1894; « The Tree of Influence » of 1895; « Orchard »; etc.

(8) - V. Pica, op. cit., page 223.

(9) - G. C. Argan, « L'Arte Moderna 1770/1970 », Sansoni, 1970, page 235.

(10) - S. Tschudi Madsen, « Art Nouveau », World University Library, 1967, pages 124-125.

(11) - Nikolaus Pevsner, « The Sources of Modern Architecture and Design », Thames & Hudson, page 140.

(12) - N. Pevsner, op. cit., page 140.

(13) - N. Pevsner, op. cit., page 143.

(14) - N. Pevsner, op. cit., page 144.

(15) - « Pan », 1895; « Die Jugend », 1896; « Simplizissimus », 1896; « Art et décoration », « L'Art décoratif », « Dekorative Kunst », « Deutsche Kunst und Dekoration », « Zeitschrift für Innendekoration », all in 1897, and finally « Ver Sacrum » and « Kunst und Kunst-Handwerk », 1898.

(16) - « The Studio », quoted by Hors-Herbert Kossatz in « Studio International », January, 1971, page 12.

(17) - « The Studio », from « Studio International », cit., page 13.

(18) - Idem.

(19) - Ludwig von Hevesi, in « Studio International », cit., page 16.

(20) - Idem.

(21) - Richard Muther, in « Studio International », cit., page 16.

(22) - T. Howarth, op. cit., page 168.

(23) - Mario Amaya, « Art Nouveau », Dutton Vista, London, 1966, page 156.

(24) - R. Macleod, op. cit., page 156.

Abbreviations

Young	*Charles Rennie Mackintosh: Architecture, Design and Painting,* 1968 Introduction and catalogue by Andrew McLaren Young
GSA booklet	*Charles Rennie Mackintosh and the Glasgow School of Art,* with text by D. P. Bliss, 1961
GSA F booklet	Charles Rennie Mackintosh, *Furniture,* 1968
Howarth	Thomas Howarth, *Charles Rennie Mackintosh and the Modern Movement,* 1952
Macleod	Robert Macleod, *Charles Rennie Mackintosh,* 1968
Pevsner (1)	Nikolaus Pevsner, *Charles R. Mackintosh,* 1950
Pevsner (2)	Nikolaus Pevsner, *Studies in Art, Architecture and Design,* 1968
Pevsner (3)	Nikolaus Pevsner, *The Sources of Modern Architecture and Design,* 1968
Pica	Vittorio Pica, *L'Arte decorativa all'Esposizione di Torino 1902,* 1903
Schmutzler	R. Schmutzler, *Art Nouveau,* 1964
Saltire	*Exhibition of Works by Charles Rennie Mackintosh,* Saltire Society and Arts Council of Great Britain, Edinburgh 1953

Catalogue of the Chairs

1. Low Back Armchair for Smoking Room, Argyle Street Tearooms (1897)
2. Armchair with High Back, Argyle Street Tearooms (1897)
3. Chair with Oval Backrail, Argyle Street Tearooms (1897)
4. Easy Chair for the Ladies' Reading Room, Argyle Street Tearooms (1897-98)
5. Armchair (1), Board Room, Glasgow School of Art (1900)
6. Armchair (2), Board Room, Glasgow School of Art (1900)
7. Chair with High Back, Ingram Street Tearooms (1900)
8. Chair with Medium Back, Ingram Street Tearooms (1900)
9. Chair with Low Back, Ingram Street Tearooms (1900)
10. Armchair with Tapering Back, Front Hall of Windyhill (1900)
11. Chair painted white, Mains Street Flat (1900)
12. Armchair with Low Back, Mains Street Flat (1900)
13. Armchair for Principal Bedroom, Westdel, Queen's Place (1901)
14. Lug Chair for Mains Street Flat (1901)
15. Chair painted white and upholstered in linen, Turin Exhibition and Wärndorfer Musik Salon, Vienna (1902)
16. Armchair painted white and upholstered in linen, Turin Exhibition (1902)
17. Armchair for Entrance Hall, Hill House, Helensburgh (1902)
18. Chair with High Back, Bedroom, Hill House, Helensburgh (1902)
19. Chair with Low Back, chequered vertical strips, Hous' Hill (1903)
20. Chair for Dining Room, Willow Tearooms (1904)
21. Chair painted silver with High Back, Room de Luxe, Willow Tearooms (1904)
22. Curved Lattice Back Chair, Willow Tearooms (1904)
23. Chair for Waitress, Ingram Street Tearooms (Grosvenor Restaurant, 1904)
24. Chair with chequered vertical strips, Bedroom, Hous' Hill (1904)
25. Chair for Waitress (1), from Ingram Street Tearooms (1907)
26. Chair for Waitress (2), from Ingram Street Tearooms (1907)
27. Chair with Low Fretwork Back, Ingram Street Tearooms (1910)

1/2 Low and High Back Armchairs for Smoking Room (tub-chair), Argyle Street Tearooms (1897)

1   Oak stained: 85,6 x 63 x 47 cm
     (33¾ x 24¾ x 18½ ins.)
2   Oak stained: 129,4 x 63 x 47 cm
     (51¼ x 24¾ x 18½ ins.)
Repr: *The Studio*, XXXIX, n° 163-1906 pp. 32-6; Howarth, pls. 13, 49/B; Schmutzler, p. 247.

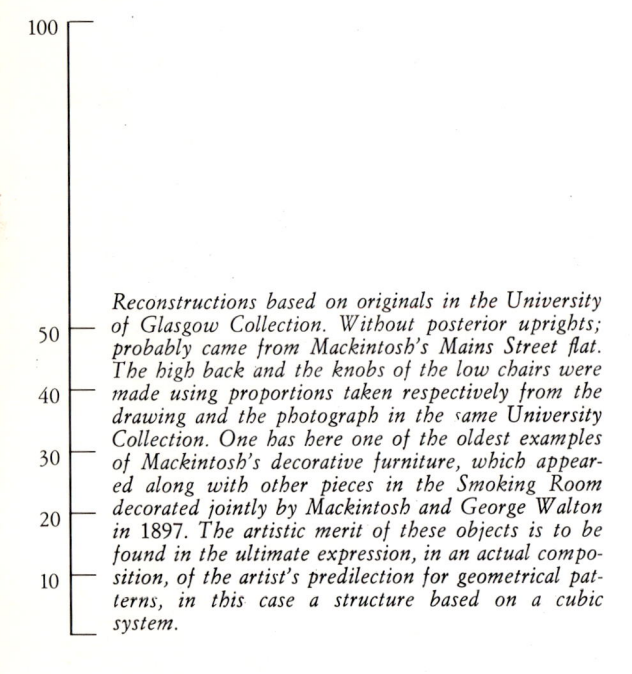

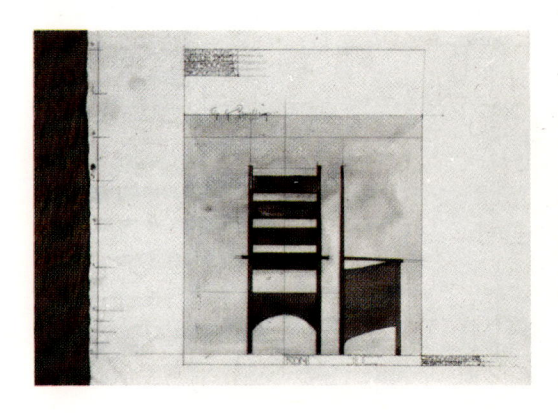

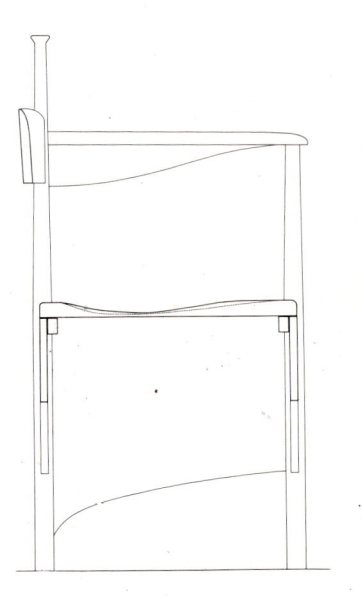

Reconstructions based on originals in the University of Glasgow Collection. Without posterior uprights; probably came from Mackintosh's Mains Street flat. The high back and the knobs of the low chairs were made using proportions taken respectively from the drawing and the photograph in the same University Collection. One has here one of the oldest examples of Mackintosh's decorative furniture, which appeared along with other pieces in the Smoking Room decorated jointly by Mackintosh and George Walton in 1897. The artistic merit of these objects is to be found in the ultimate expression, in an actual composition, of the artist's predilection for geometrical patterns, in this case a structure based on a cubic system.

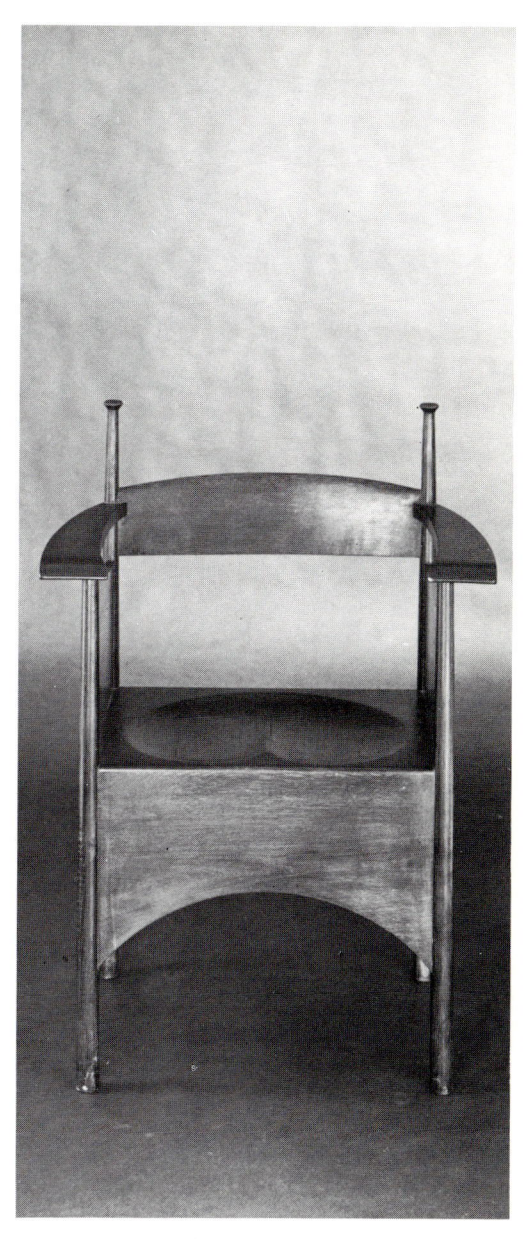

31

SCHOOL OF THE MUSEUM
OF FINE ARTS · BOSTON

**3 Chair with Oval Backrail,
Argyle Street Tearooms (1897)**

Oak with horsehair seat: 136 x 50,5 x 45,8 cm (53½ x 19¾ x 18 ins.)
Exh: Vienna, *Sezession*, 1900; London, Arts Council, *Art Nouveau in Britain*, 1965; London, Royal Academy of Arts, *Vienna Secession*, 1971.
Repr: *Ver Sacrum,* 1900/24, p. 385; *Dekorative Kunst,* IV, 1901, p. 175; *The Studio Special Number,* 1901, pp. 110-111; Howarth, pls. 13A, 14A, 15A, 59A, 59C; Macleod, p. 99; GSA booklet, pls. 7, 17B.

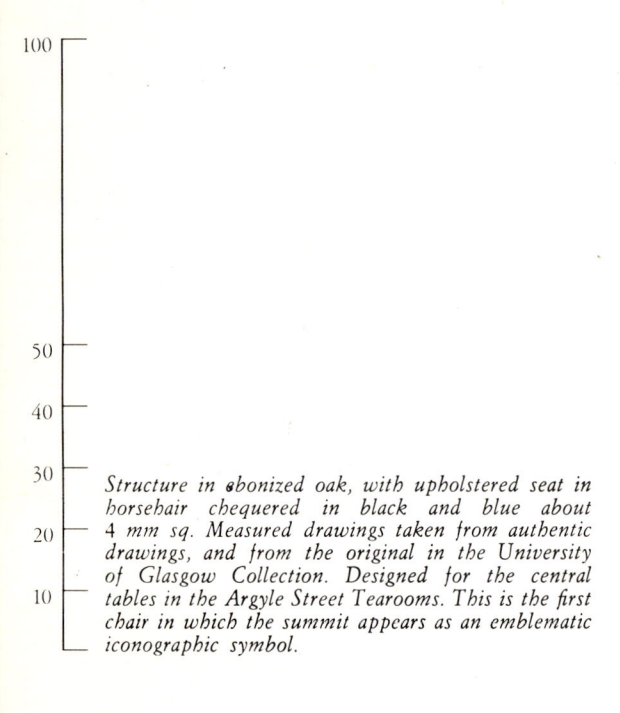

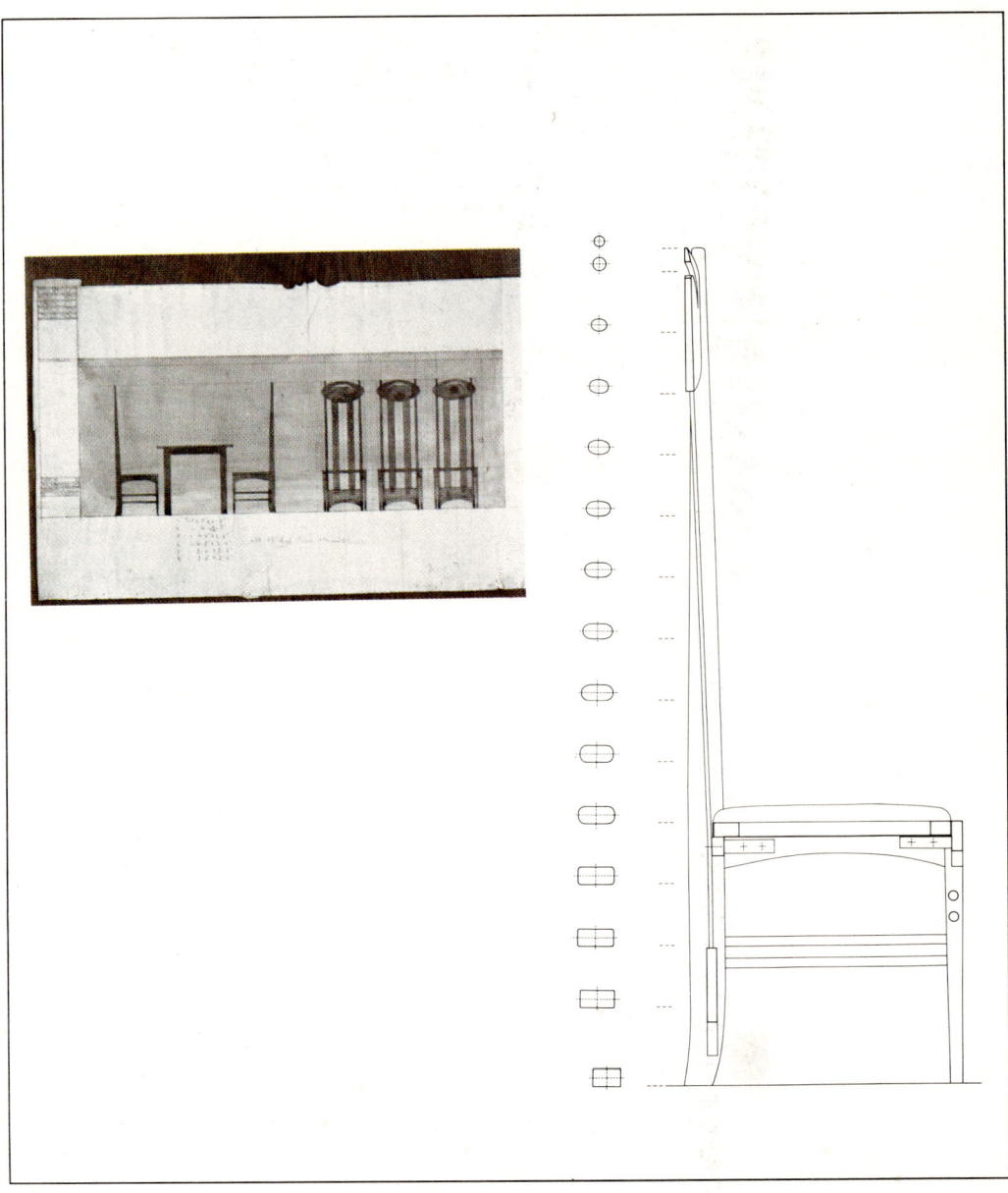

Structure in ebonized oak, with upholstered seat in horsehair chequered in black and blue about 4 mm sq. Measured drawings taken from authentic drawings, and from the original in the University of Glasgow Collection. Designed for the central tables in the Argyle Street Tearooms. This is the first chair in which the summit appears as an emblematic iconographic symbol.

33

**4   Easy Chair for the Ladies' Reading Room, Miss Cranston's Tearooms
(probably in Argyle Street, 1897-98)**

Oak stained with inlay, upholstered seat with horsehair: 122 x 66 x 61,5 cm
(48 x 26 x 24 ins.)
Repr: GSA booklet, pl. 9.

An easy chair, as the designer himself tells us, for a reading room. In stained oak with a large emblem carved on the sides, its seat and back upholstered in horsehair. The replica, reproduced from measured drawings taken from the original in the Mackintosh Room in the Glasgow School of Art, has been upholstered in the same horsehair material as the original. However, in an original drawing dated 1903-5, from the University of Glasgow Collection, the same chair is shown upholstered in oatmeal-coloured embroidered linen. Austere, massive but none the less elegant, this chair echoes the structure and the particular feeling of the chairs produced towards the end of the century. This chair cannot, however, be grouped with these because of the lack of the strong tensile curves which characterize the chairs of that period.

34

SCHOOL OF THE MUSEUM
OF FINE ARTS · BOSTON

**5/6 Armchairs for Board Room,
Glasgow School of Art (1900)**

Oak with horsehair seat:
5   75,3 x 56 x 46 cm (29$^5/_8$ x 22 x 18$^1/_8$ ins.)
6   81,2 x 58,5 x 50 cm (32 x 23 x 18$^5/_8$ ins.)
Repr: Macleod, p. 60; GSA booklet, pls. 1, 15.

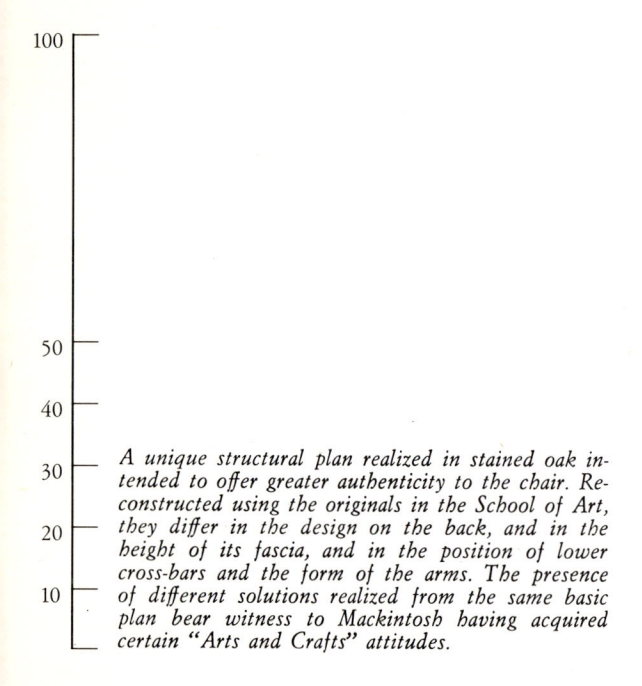

A unique structural plan realized in stained oak intended to offer greater authenticity to the chair. Reconstructed using the originals in the School of Art, they differ in the design on the back, and in the height of its fascia, and in the position of lower cross-bars and the form of the arms. The presence of different solutions realized from the same basic plan bear witness to Mackintosh having acquired certain "Arts and Crafts" attitudes.

37

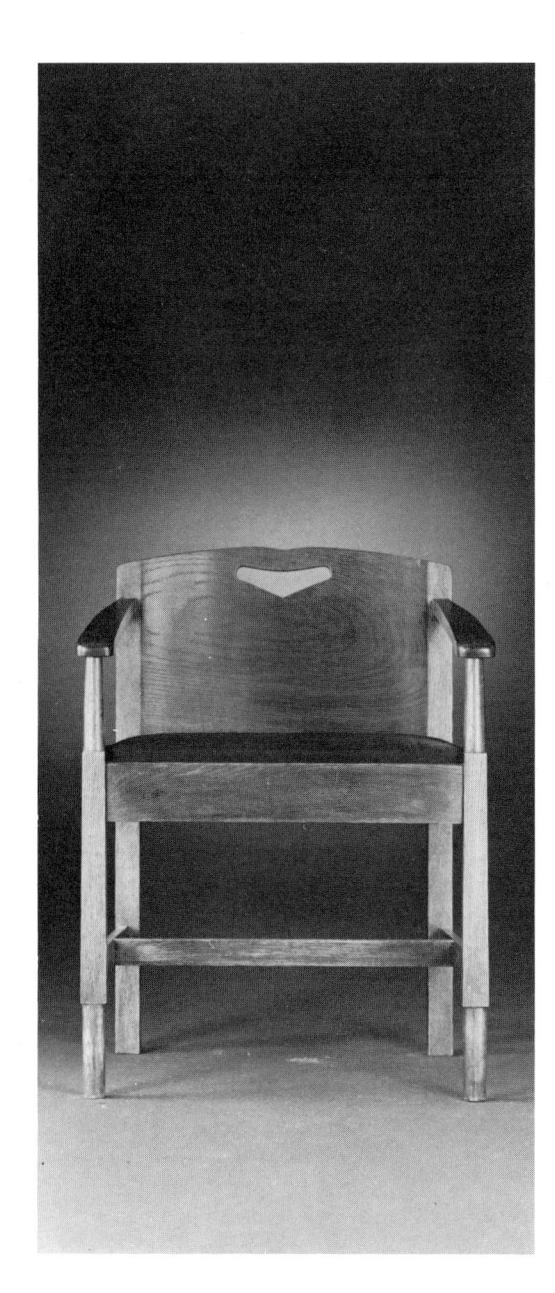

5/6 Armchairs for Board Room,
     Glasgow School of Art (1900)

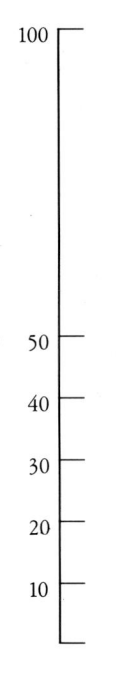

39

7   **Chair with High Back,
Ingram Street Tearooms (1900)**

Oak with fabric seat: 151,8 x 48 x 44 cm
(59³/₄ x 19 x 17¹/₄ ins.)
Repr: Howarth, p. 104; Schmutzler, p. 256; GSA booklet, pls. 6, 9B.

8   **Chair with Medium Back,
Ingram Street Tearooms (1900)**

Oak with fabric seat: 106 x 48 x 44 cm
(41³/₄ x 18⁷/₈ x 17¹/₄ ins.)
Repr: Howarth, pl. 50A; GSA booklet, pl. 5.

9   **Chair with Low Back,
Ingram Street Tearooms (1900)**

Oak with fabric seat: 84 x 48,5 x 44,5 cm
(33 x 19¹/₈ x 17¹/₂ ins.)
Repr: Macleod, p. 137.

11   **Chair for Mains Street Flat
(white painted version
of Ingram Street Tearooms, Chair n° 7)**

Oak, painted white, with fabric seat:
151,8 x 48 x 44 cm
(59³/₄ x 19 x 17¹/₄ ins.)
Repr: *The Studio Special Number,* 1901, p. 113;
Howarth, pls. 12A, 13A.

Structure in stained oak, seats upholstered in cloth. Reconstructions were made by measuring the shape and size of the originals in the University of Glasgow Collection, and in the School of Art, Glasgow. This set expresses a profoundly logical and rational system, and maintains a rare elegance in similar versions differing in the height of the back. Mackintosh's neo-Gothic cypher becomes apparent here, in a rigidly symmetrical, geometrical scheme. Over and above any stylistic figuration represented in the three examples, one is aware of the high backs, placed in the centre of the room around a table, running together to create islands of privacy.

Made in oak painted white, based on the original in the University of Glasgow Collection and intended for the Mains Street flat. This chair, which is recognized as one of the Ingram series, underlines, with the different cosmetic treatment of white paint and little glass windows, one of Mackintosh's first relationships with Art Nouveau.

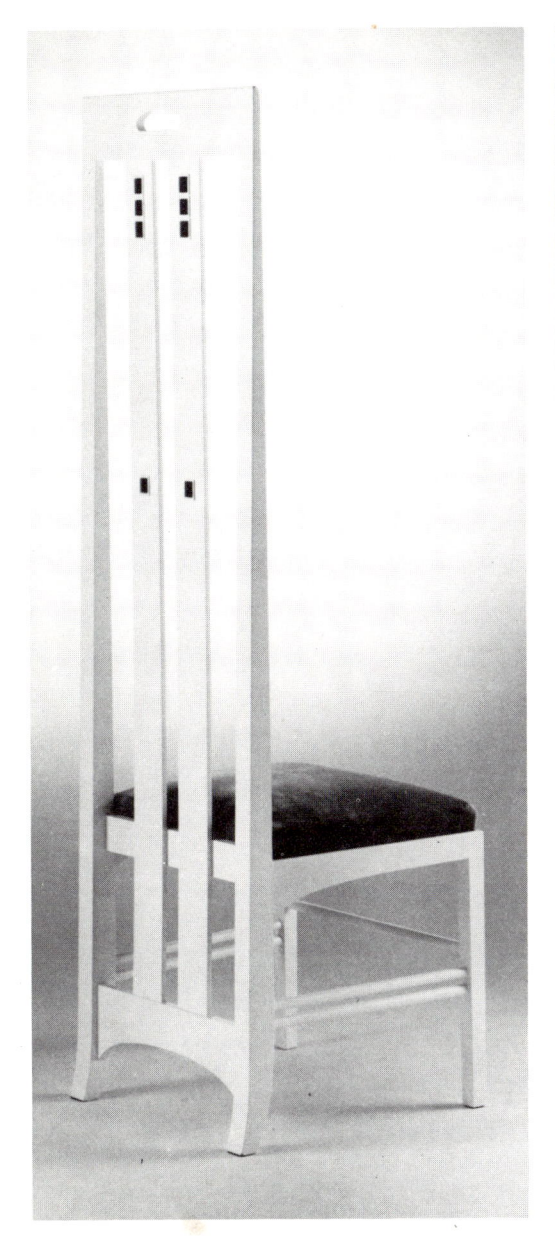

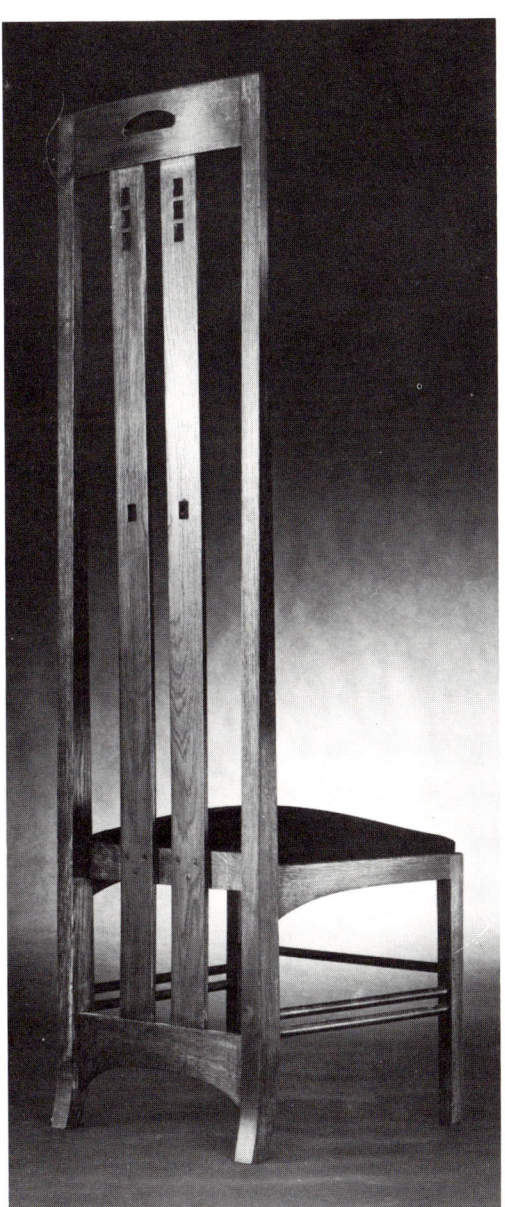

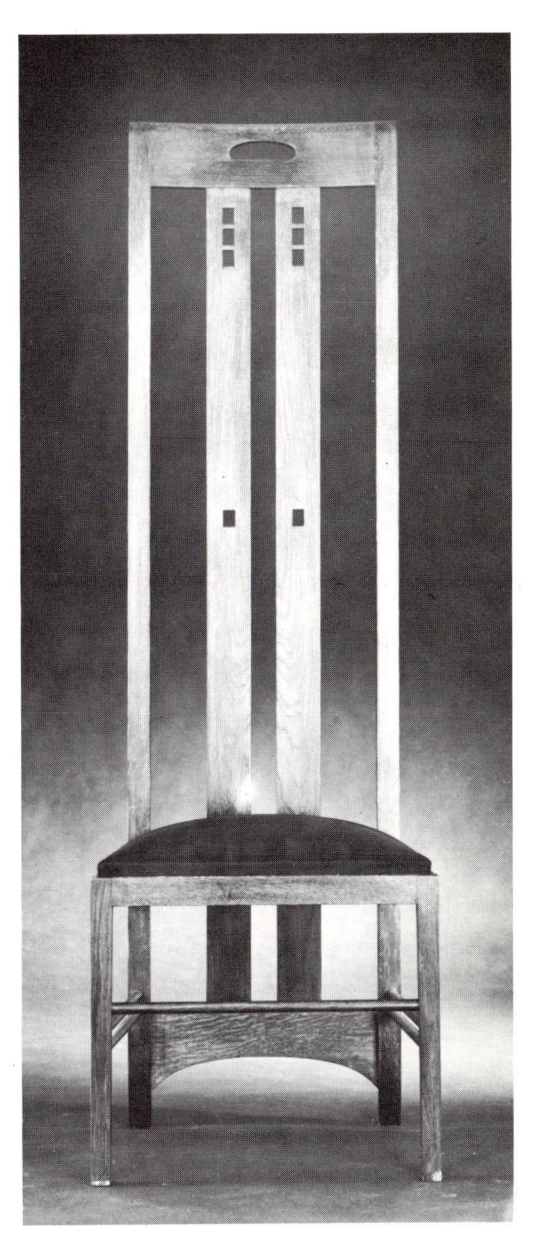

41

SCHOOL OF THE MUSEUM
OF FINE ARTS · BOSTON

42

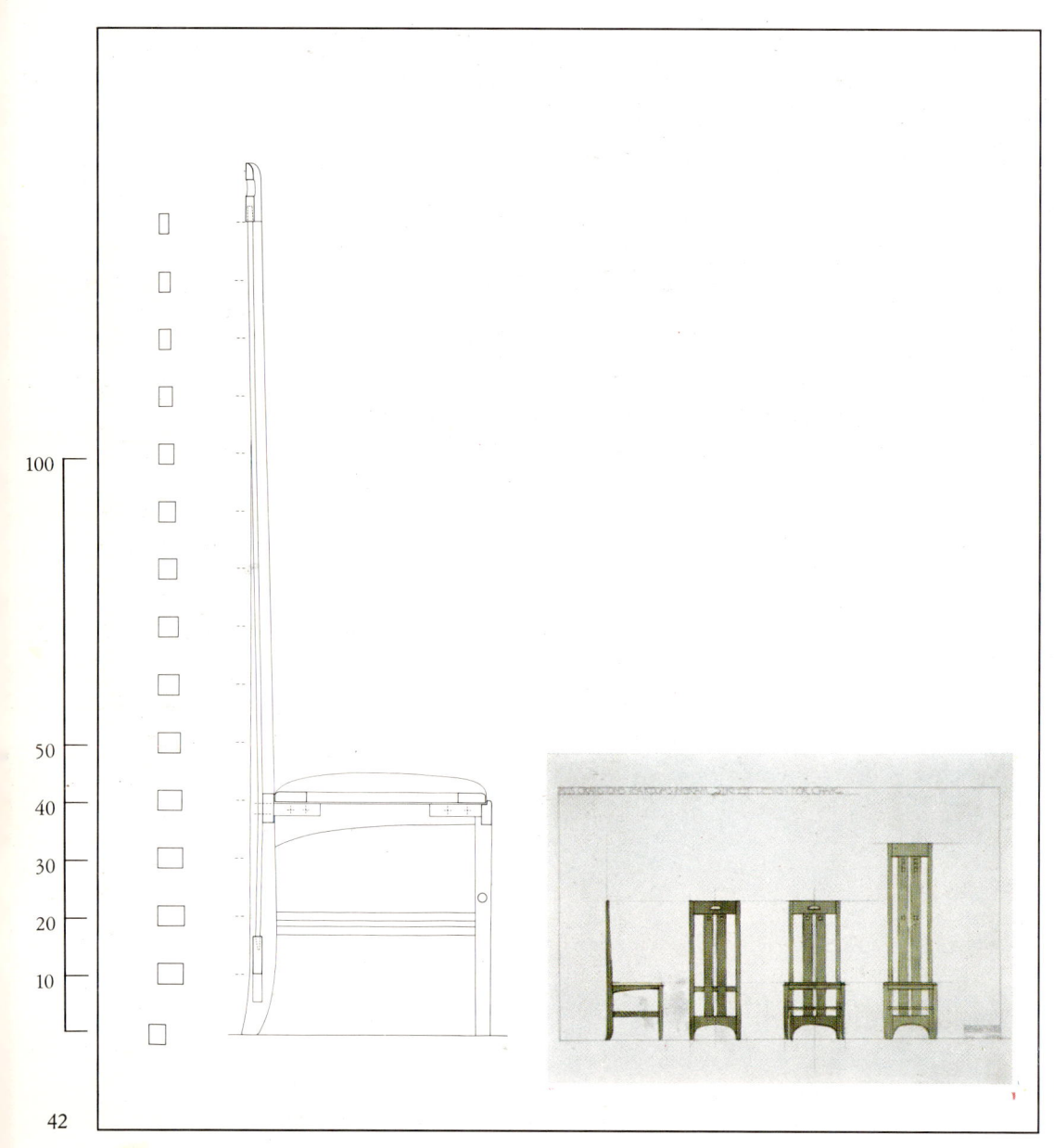

43

10   **Armchair with Tapering Back, Front Hall of Windyhill (1900)**

Oak with rush seat: 133,5 x 73 x 54,5 cm (52½ x 28¾ x 21½ ins.)
Repr: *Dekorative Kunst*, V, 1902, p. 197: Muthesius, *Das Englische Haus*, 1, 1904, p. 200; Howarth, pl. 35B; Pevsner (2), p. 102: *Scottish Art Review*, XI, n° 4, 1968, p. 13; Young, pl. 21A.

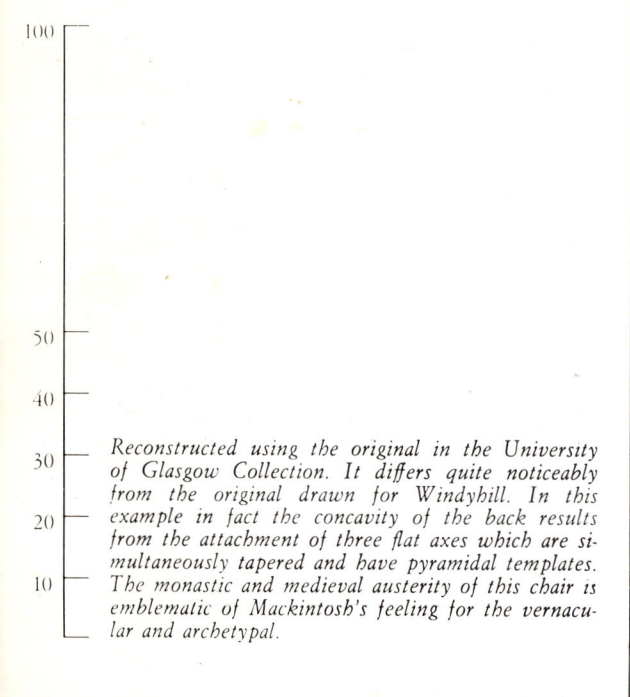

Reconstructed using the original in the University of Glasgow Collection. It differs quite noticeably from the original drawn for Windyhill. In this example in fact the concavity of the back results from the attachment of three flat axes which are simultaneously tapered and have pyramidal templates. The monastic and medieval austerity of this chair is emblematic of Mackintosh's feeling for the vernacular and archetypal.

45

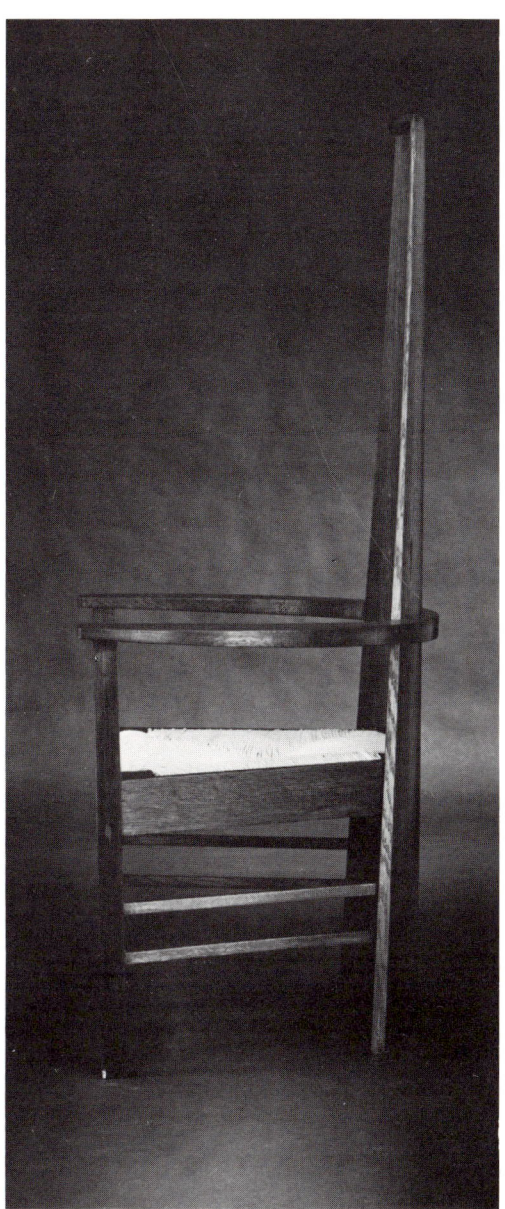

**12　Armchair with Low Back,
　　Mains Street Flat (1900)**

Oak with upholstered seat: 88,5 x 64,5 x 61 cm (35 x 25½ x 24 ins.)
Repr: *The Studio Special Number*, 1901, p. 113; Muthesius, *Das Englische Haus*, 1, 1904, p. 188; Howarth, pls. 12A, 13A.

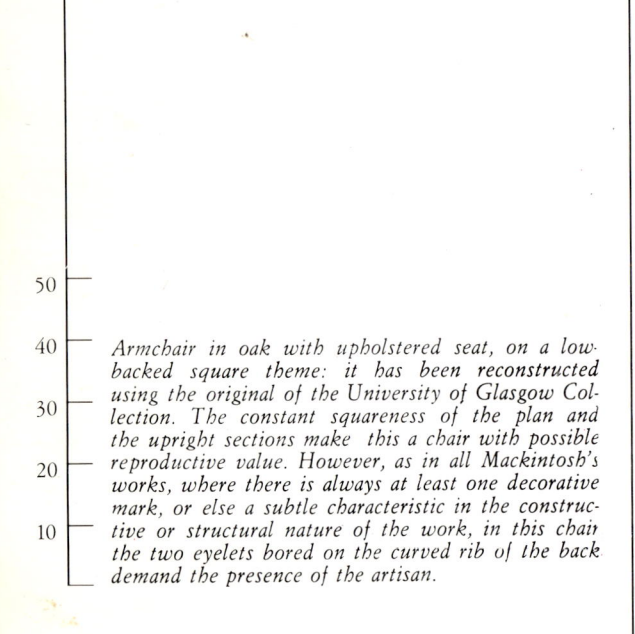

Armchair in oak with upholstered seat, on a low-backed square theme: it has been reconstructed using the original of the University of Glasgow Collection. The constant squareness of the plan and the upright sections make this a chair with possible reproductive value. However, as in all Mackintosh's works, where there is always at least one decorative mark, or else a subtle characteristic in the constructive or structural nature of the work, in this chair the two eyelets bored on the curved rib of the back demand the presence of the artisan.

47

13   **Armchair for Principal Bedroom, Westdel, Queen's Place (1901)**

Oak, dark brown stain finish with horsehair seat: 97,3 x 57x 45,5 cm (38¼ x 17¾ ins.)

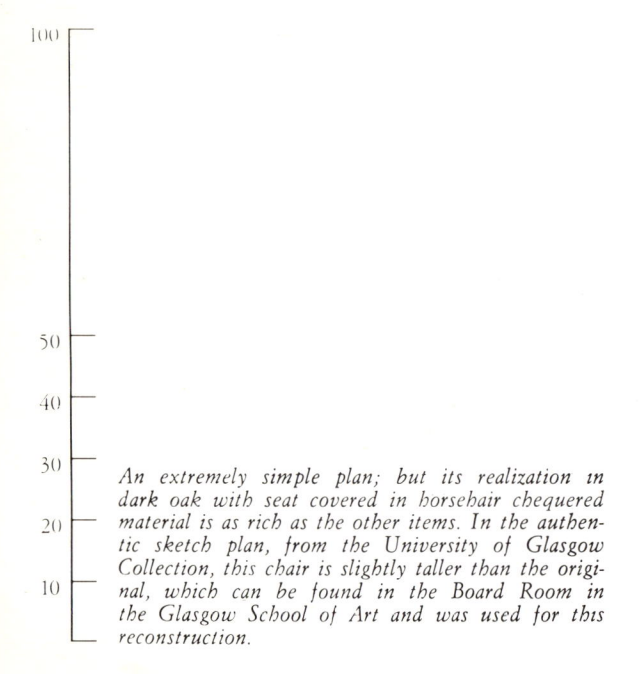

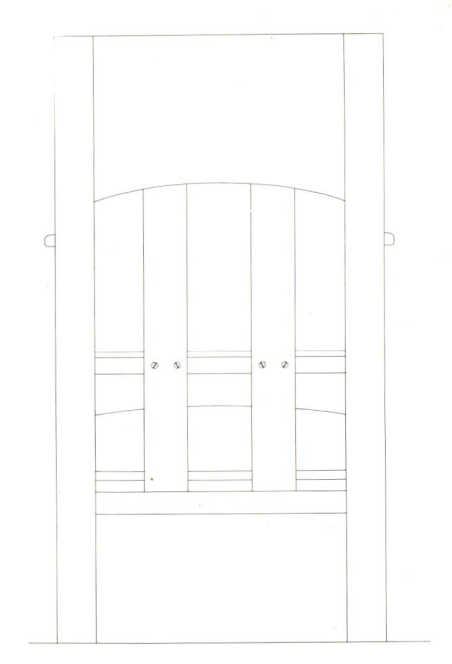

An extremely simple plan; but its realization in dark oak with seat covered in horsehair chequered material is as rich as the other items. In the authentic sketch plan, from the University of Glasgow Collection, this chair is slightly taller than the original, which can be found in the Board Room in the Glasgow School of Art and was used for this reconstruction.

48

49

14 Lug Chair for Mains Street Flat (1901)

Stained oak with inlay, upholstered seat and back with oatmeal-coloured fabric:
129,5 x 72,6 x 70,4 cm
(51 x 28½ x 27¾ ins.)
Repr: Howarth, pl. 12A; Young, pl. 32.

Lug chairs in stained oak with carved emblems with the characteristic design which became known as the Glasgow Style. It is upholstered in oatmeal-coloured fabric with insets in ribbon entrelac. To permit easier movement, it is mounted on castors hidden in the base. The semantics of its composition suggest a chair of Norse tradition still in use in remoter islands. Despi.. the simplicity of its structure, this chair illustrates better than some of the others that essential Mackintosh design quality, composed essentially of surfaces and orthogonal planes, the regular geometry of which is tempered by a simple but almost always highly stylized line. This line is sometimes a pure symbolic form mediated by archaic indigenous tones, and at other times, particularly after 1900, one can trace the influence of Art Nouveau.

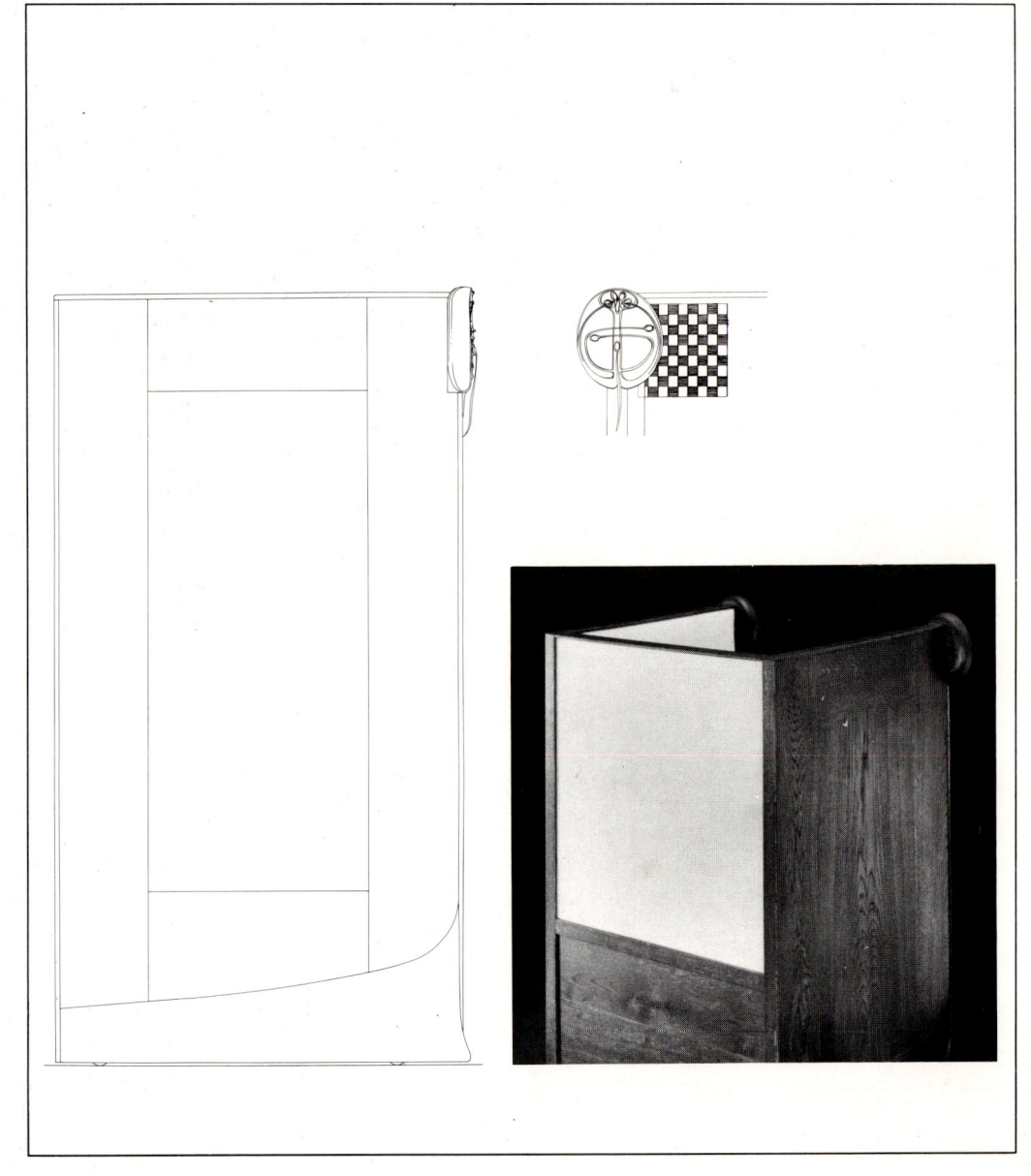

51

15 Chair painted white and upholstered in linen, Turin Exhibition and Wärndorfer Musik Salon, Vienna (1902)

Oak, painted white with stencilled canvas back: 152,4 x 67,6 x 54,6 cm (60 x 26½ x 21½ ins.)

Exh: Turin, 1902; Saltire, 1953 (bl); New York, Museum of Modern Art, 1960-1; Royal Academy of Arts, *Vienna Secession*, 1971.

Repr: *The Studio*, XXVI, 1902, p. 92; *Deutsche Kunst und Dekoration*, XII, 1902, pp. 586, 589; Pica, p. 213; *R.I.B.A. Journal*, LIII, 1946, p. 491; Howarth, pls. 12B, 64B; Schmutzler, p. 251.

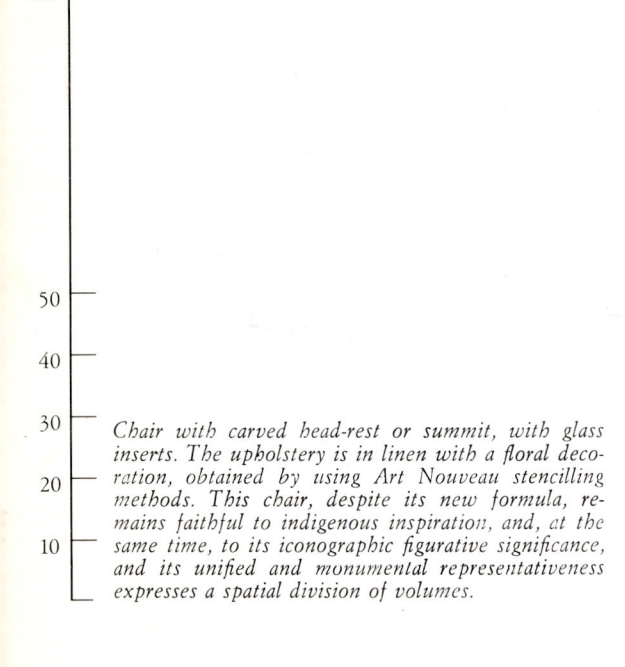

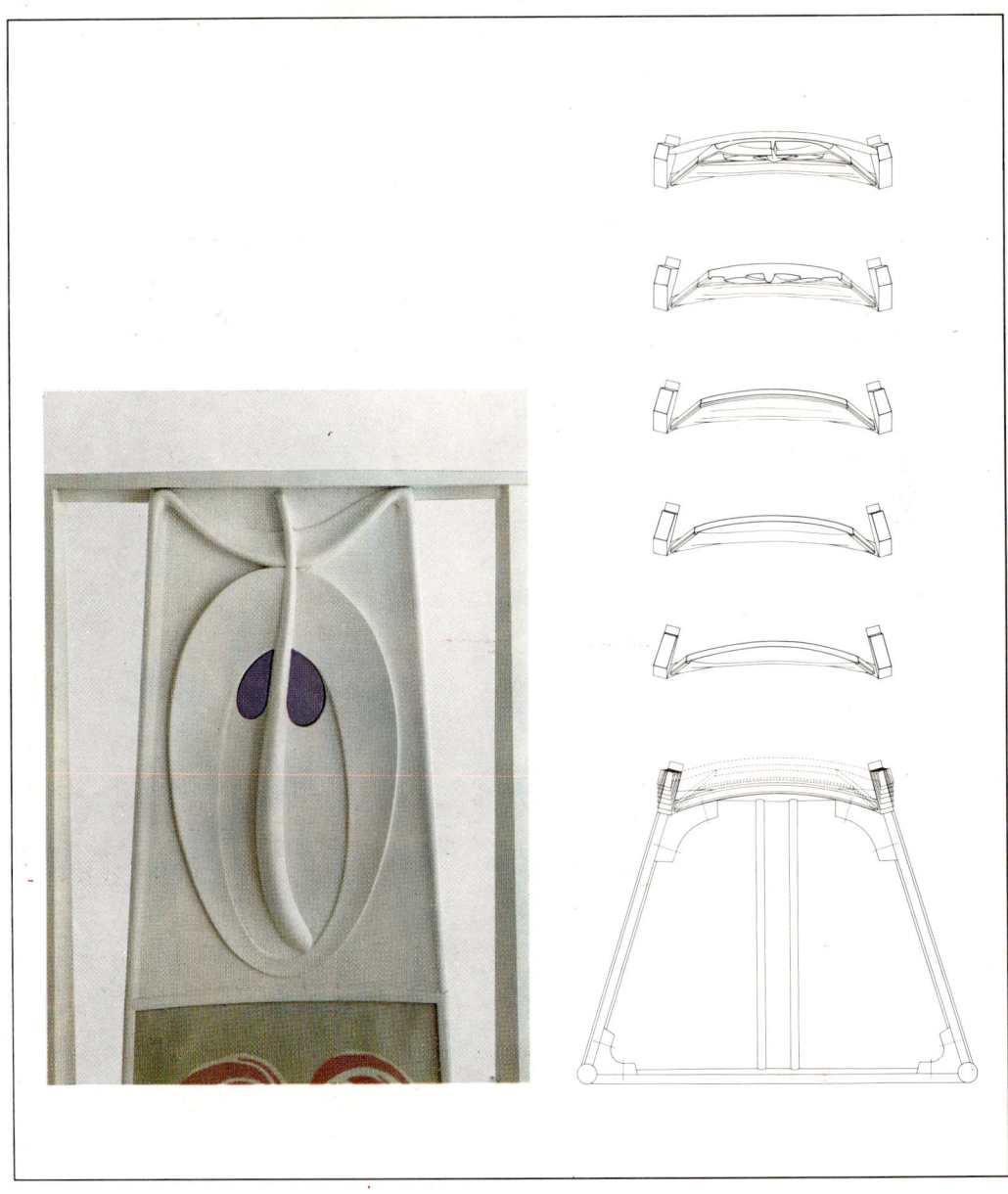

Chair with carved head-rest or summit, with glass inserts. The upholstery is in linen with a floral decoration, obtained by using Art Nouveau stencilling methods. This chair, despite its new formula, remains faithful to indigenous inspiration, and, at the same time, to its iconographic figurative significance, and its unified and monumental representativeness expresses a spatial division of volumes.

52

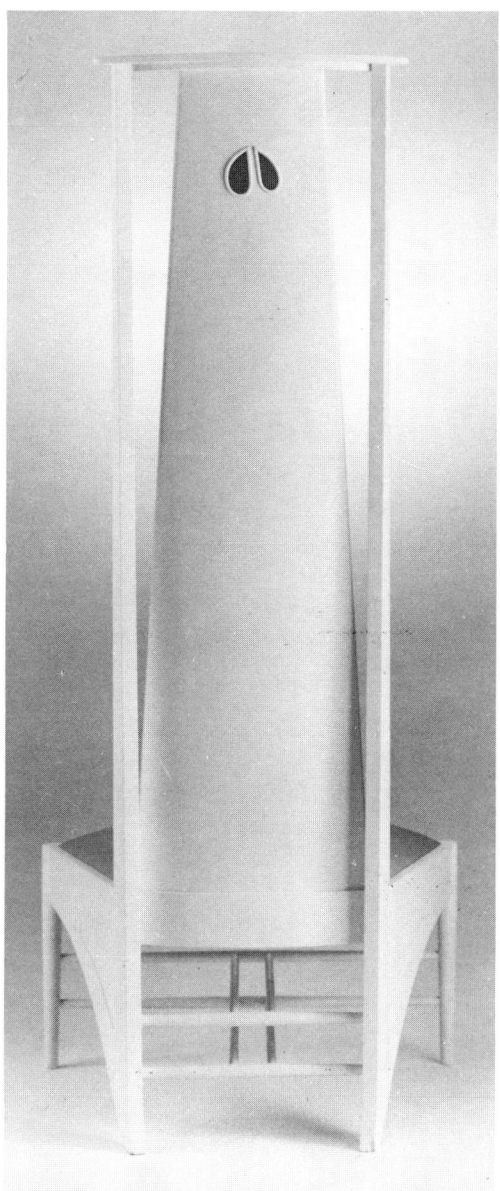

53

SCHOOL OF THE MUSEUM
OF FINE ARTS · BOSTON

16   Armchair painted white and upholstered in linen, Turin Exhibition (1902)

Oak, painted white with stencilled canvas back: 113,6 x 70,2 x 57 cm (44¾ x 27½ x 22½ ins.)

Exh: Turin, 1902; Moscow, 1903; London, V. and A., *Victorian and Edwardian Decorative Arts*, 1952; Saltire, 1953; Paris, *Sources of the 20th Century*, 1960-61; Munich, *Sezession*, 1964; Ostend, *Europe 1900*, 1967.

Repr: *The Studio*, XXVI, 1902, pp. 92, 96; *Deutsche Kunst und Dekoration*, XII, 1902, pp. 586, 589; *Mir Iskusstva*, n° 3, 1903, p. 117; *R.I.B.A. Journal*, LIII, 1946, p. 490; Howarth, pls. 16B, 64B; R. Barilli: *Il Liberty*, 1966, pl. B2; Macleod, p. 108; Pevsner (2), p. 138.

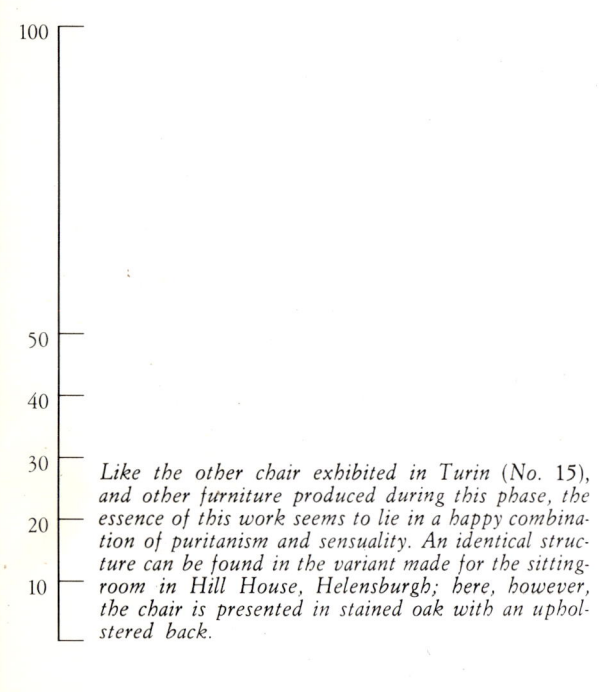

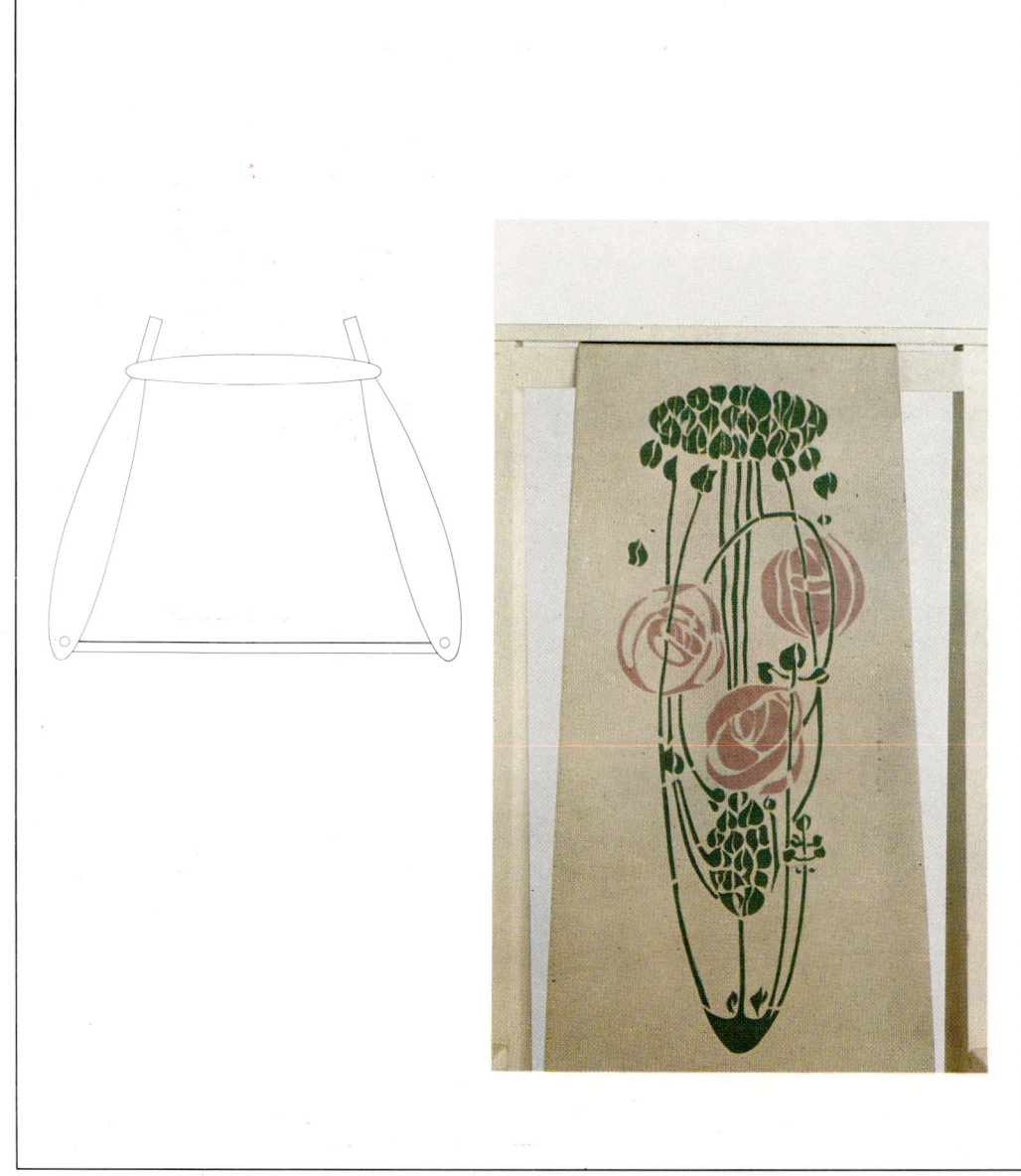

Like the other chair exhibited in Turin (No. 15), and other furniture produced during this phase, the essence of this work seems to lie in a happy combination of puritanism and sensuality. An identical structure can be found in the variant made for the sitting-room in Hill House, Helensburgh; here, however, the chair is presented in stained oak with an upholstered back.

54

55

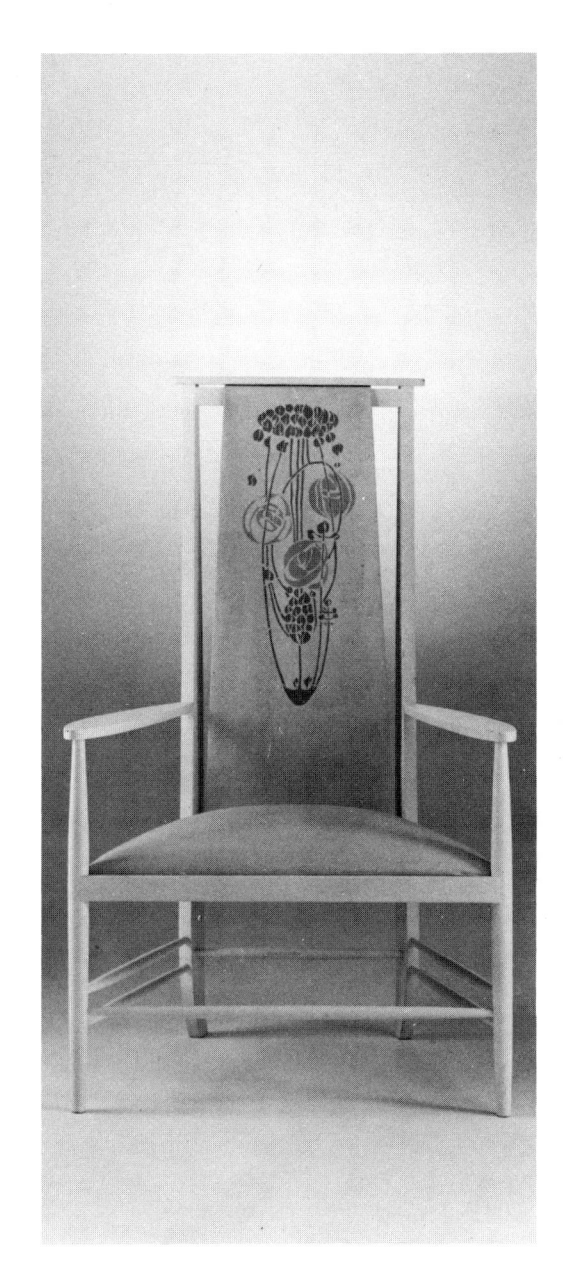

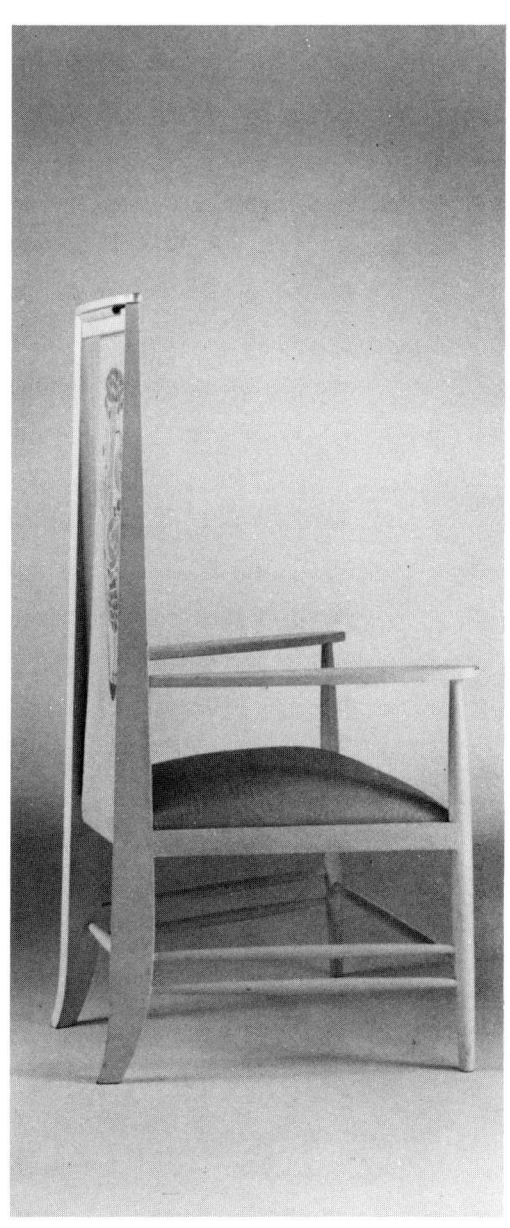

**17   Armchair for Entrance Hall,
        Hill House, Helensburgh (1902)**

Oak, in natural colour, rush seating:
73,5 x 67,4 x 57,2 cm (29 x 26½ x 22½ ins)
Repr: *Deutsche Kunst und Dekoration*, VI, 1905,
pp. 348-9; Howarth, pls. 39, 40A, 40B;
Schmutzler, p. 252.

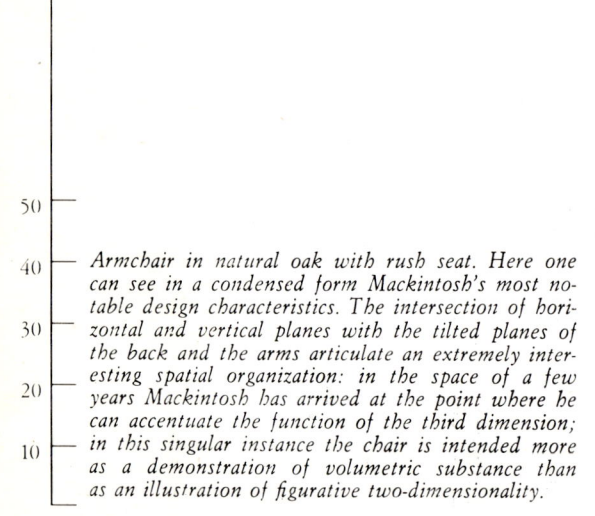

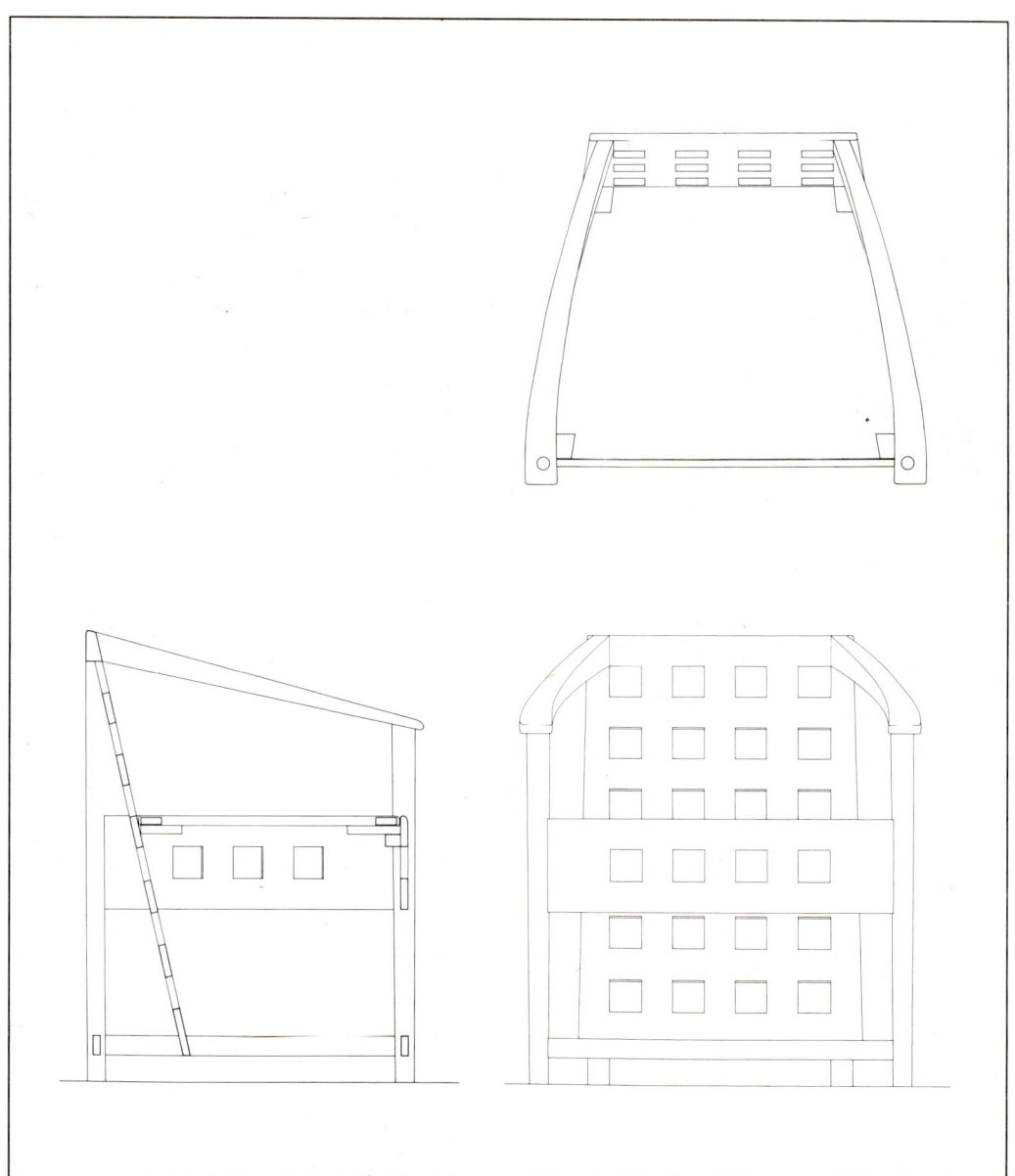

Armchair in natural oak with rush seat. Here one can see in a condensed form Mackintosh's most notable design characteristics. The intersection of horizontal and vertical planes with the tilted planes of the back and the arms articulate an extremely interesting spatial organization: in the space of a few years Mackintosh has arrived at the point where he can accentuate the function of the third dimension; in this singular instance the chair is intended more as a demonstration of volumetric substance than as an illustration of figurative two-dimensionality.

57

18 Chair with High Back (Ladderback Chair), Bedroom, Hill House, Helensburgh (1902)

Ebonized wood with upholstered seat: 140,5 x 40,5 x 33,5 cm ($55^5/_8$ x $15^3/_4$ x $13^1/_4$ ins.)
Repr: *Deutsche Kunst und Dekoration,* VI, 1905, pp. 351, 352; Pevsner (1), p. 109; Howarth, pl. 42; Macleod, pp. 90, 92; Pevsner (3), p. 153; Pevsner (2), pp. 164, 165; *Scottish Art Review,* XI, n° 4, p. 9; Young, pl. 23.

Constructed in ebonized wood, with a ladderback which is relatively high in relation to the upholstered seat. The chair from which the reconstruction was made still occupies the original position in the Hill House bedroom in Helensburgh. In this chair Mackintosh appears to have liberated himself from stylistic connotations. The iconographic presence of the head-rest or summit is less in evidence; he has placed it almost as a rational, indeed a kinetic, conclusion to the acceleration of the successive rungs; the section of the rungs and the uprights is dealt with at the extreme limit of resistance, the weight being Kg. 3. Mackintosh moves with assurance towards ornamental abstraction in this experimental design.

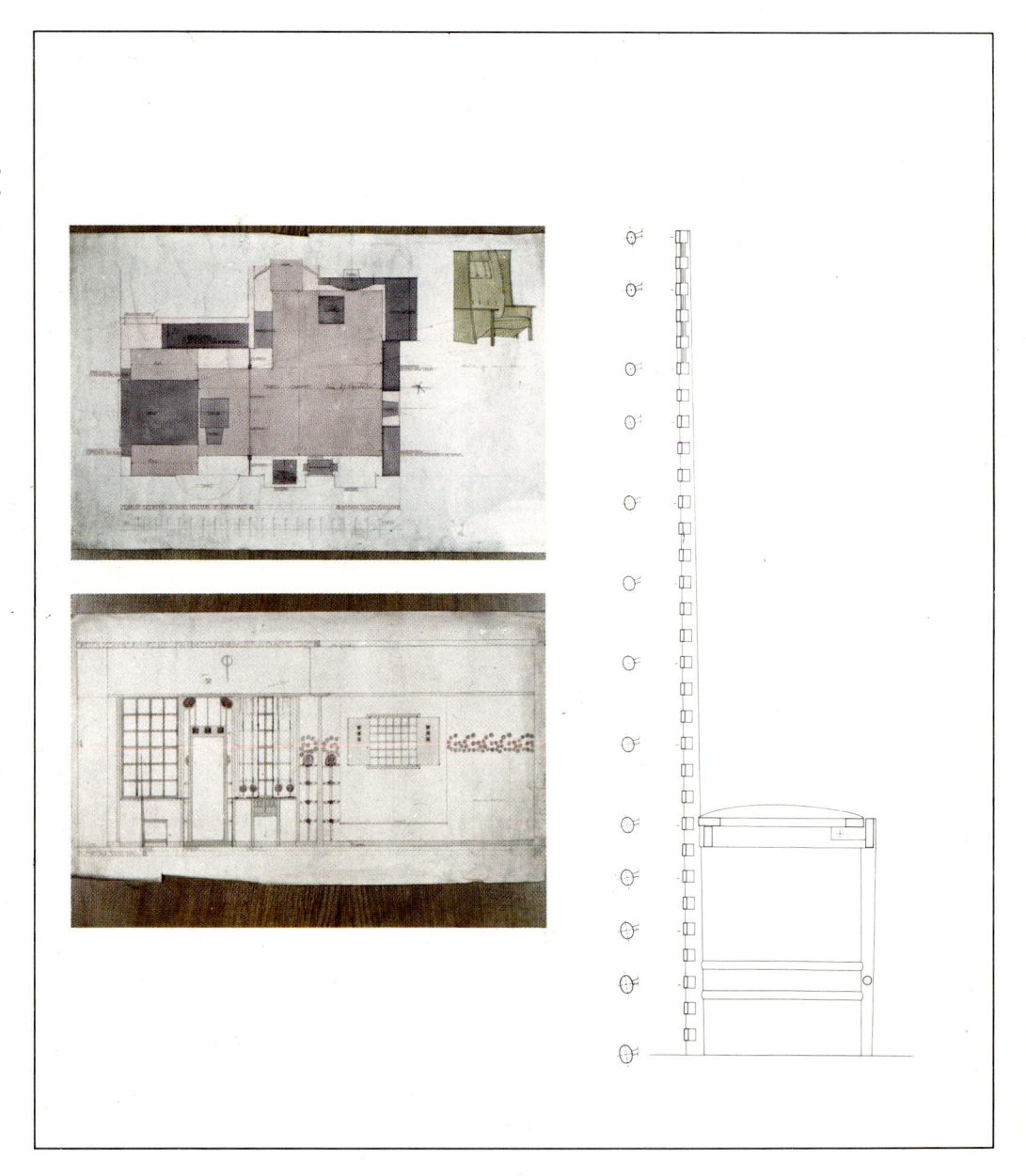

58

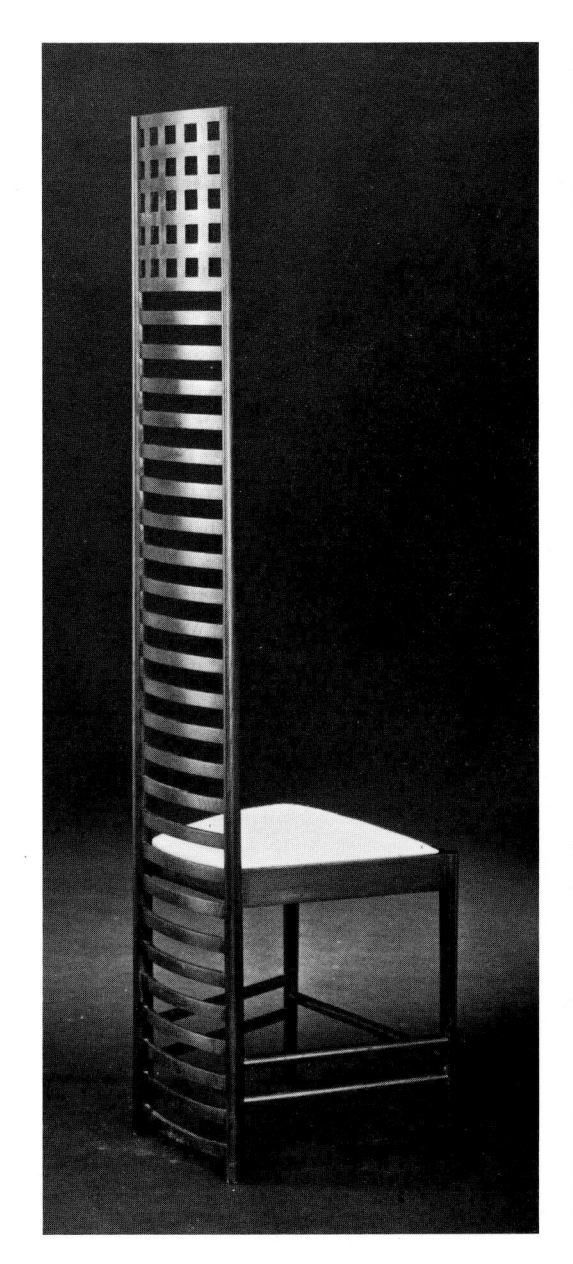

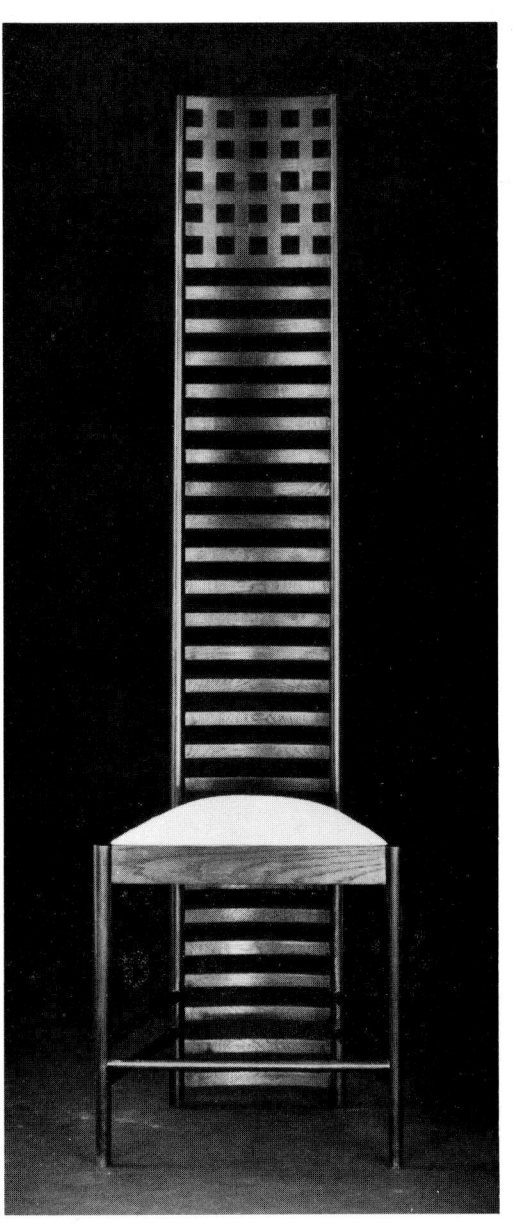

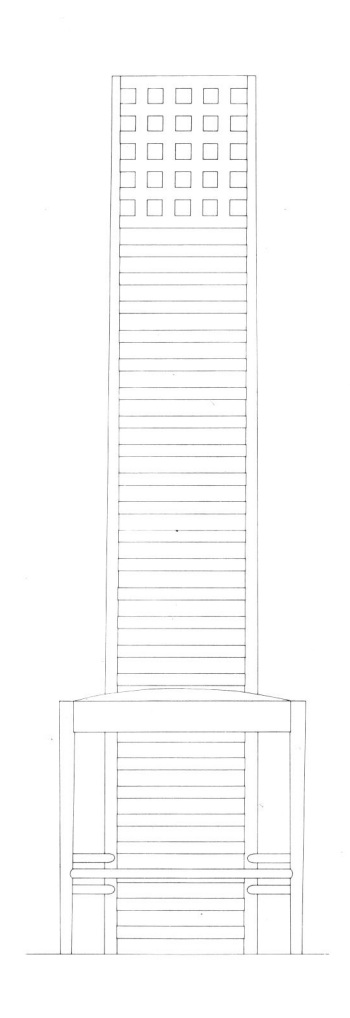

59

19 Chair with Low Back,
chequered vertical strips, Hous' Hill (1903)

Sycamore, dark brown finish, upholstered seat with corduroy: 71,5 x 43 x 35,2 cm (28$^1/_8$ x 17 x 13$^7/_8$ ins.)

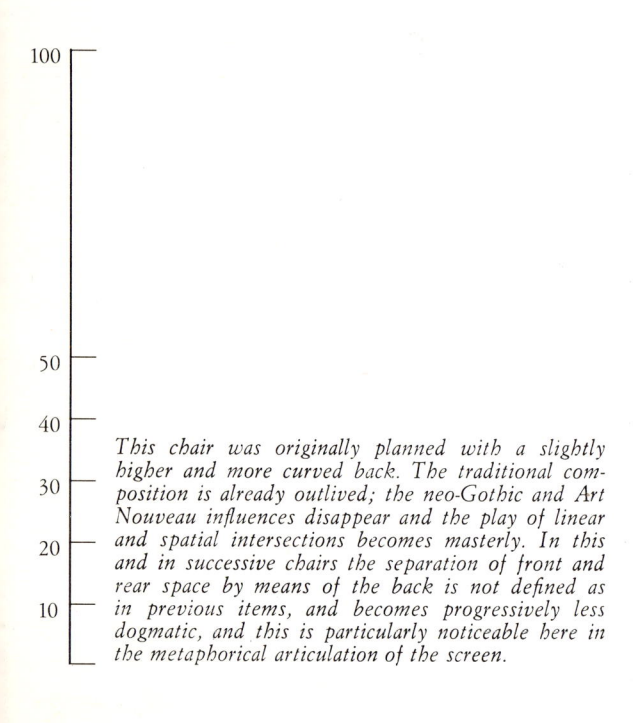

This chair was originally planned with a slightly higher and more curved back. The traditional composition is already outlived; the neo-Gothic and Art Nouveau influences disappear and the play of linear and spatial intersections becomes masterly. In this and in successive chairs the separation of front and rear space by means of the back is not defined as in previous items, and becomes progressively less dogmatic, and this is particularly noticeable here in the metaphorical articulation of the screen.

61

**20   Chair for Dining Room,
      Willow Tearooms (1904)**

Oak, dark stain finish, rush seat:
104,2 x 46 x 40 cm (41 x 18 x 15¾ ins.)
Repr: *Dekorative Kunst*, VIII, 1905, p. 261; Howarth, pls. 54, 55A, 55B, 56A; Schmutzler, p. 249; GSA booklet, pls. 8, 10.

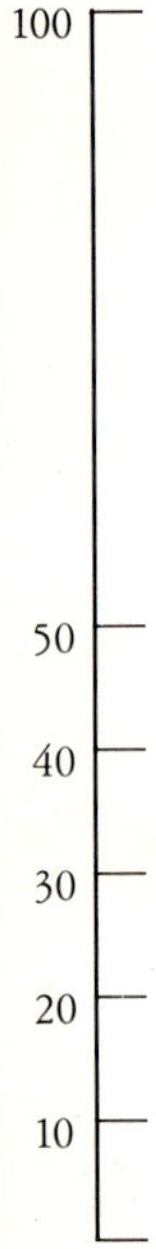

Chair for Dining Room of the Willow Tearooms with a ladderback and a rush seat. The reconstruction, like the original in the Glasgow School of Art, is in stained oak. The rear traverse on the top of the back was added later to strengthen the chair. This is the first and perhaps the only item Mackintosh produced without decorative figurations, and it represents a most important summit in the evolutionary art of the master designer. The virtuosity of the volume is created by the rhythmic division of the ribs.

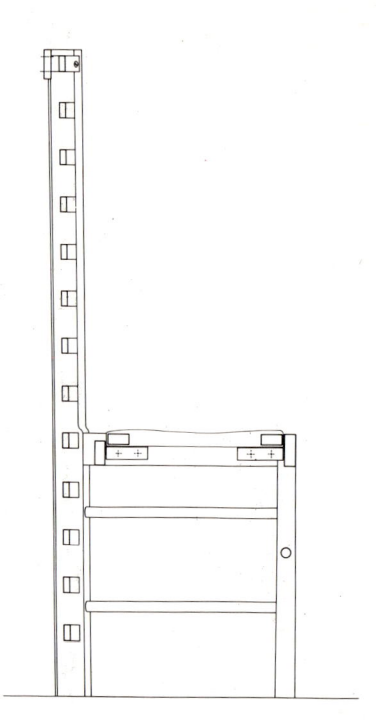

63

SCHOOL OF THE MUSEUM
OF FINE ARTS • BOSTON

**21 Chair with High Back,
Room de Luxe, Willow Tearooms (1904)**

Oak, painted silver and upholstered with purple coloured silk-velvet:
137,2 x 49 x 48,4 cm (54 x 19¼ x 19 ins.)
Repr: Howarth, pl. 57A.

As it was not possible to obtain an original, the reconstruction was made on the basis of photographs and drawings. This chair, with its rigid design with Art Nouveau overtones, is one of the most conspicuous examples of the complexity of Mackintosh's personality, which showed a well-calibrated dynamic fusion between the formal rigour of Celtic and perhaps Renaissance elements, and the typical licentiousness of the new mode: its curves, which twine and unfold like branches, contrast the hieratic verticality of the back, a back which in its turn moulds itself like symbolic drapery. Placed as a pivot in the centre of the Room de Luxe, these chairs with their tall elegance create an extraordinary centrifugal space, which is further underlined by the repetition of the frieze running around the walls.

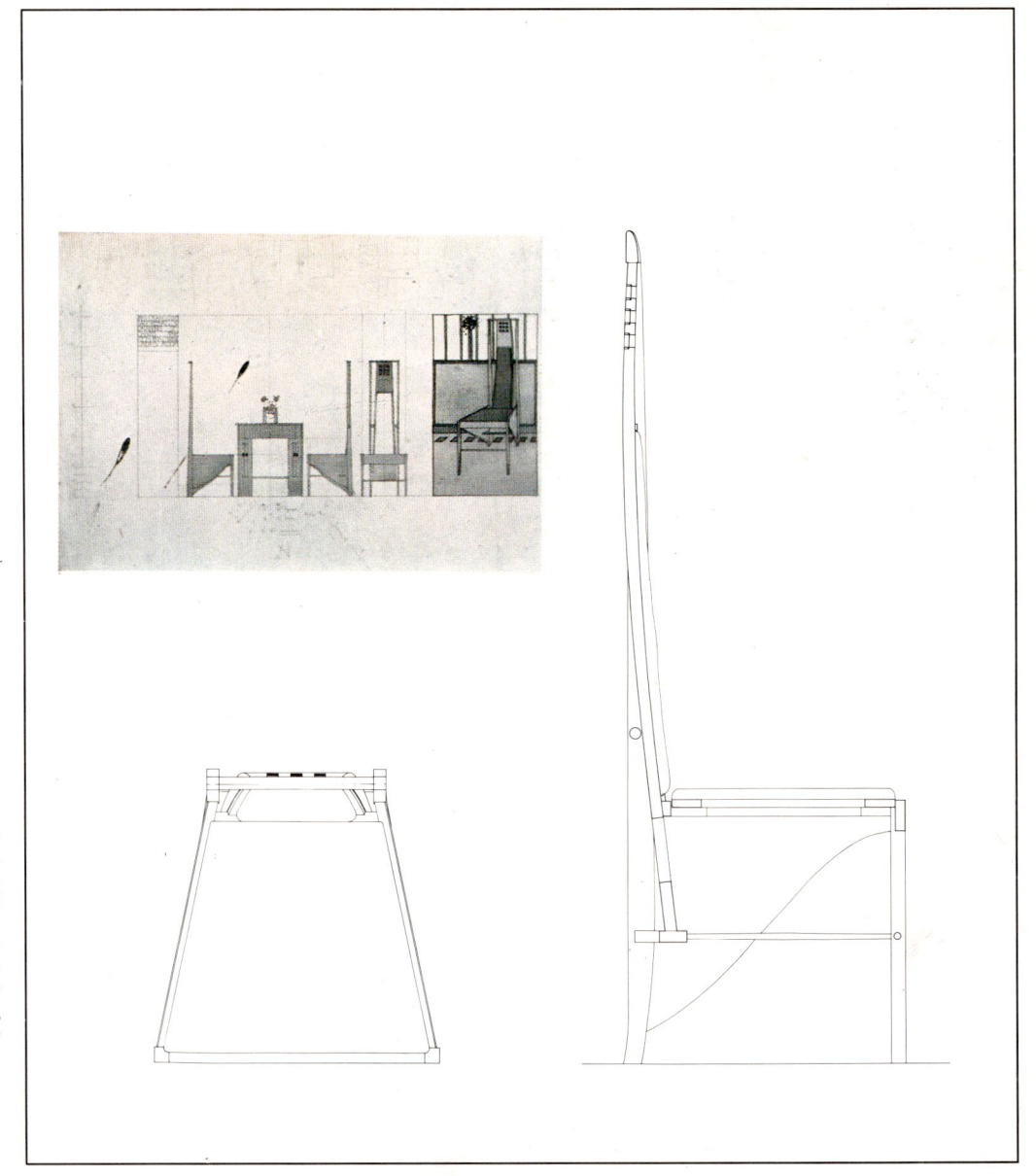

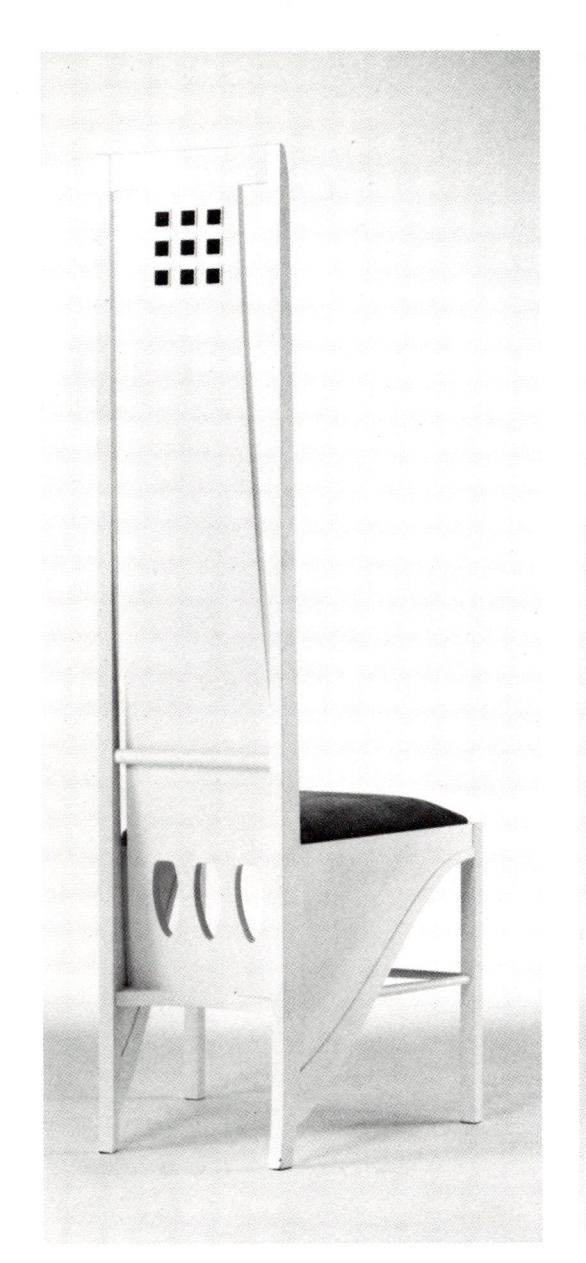

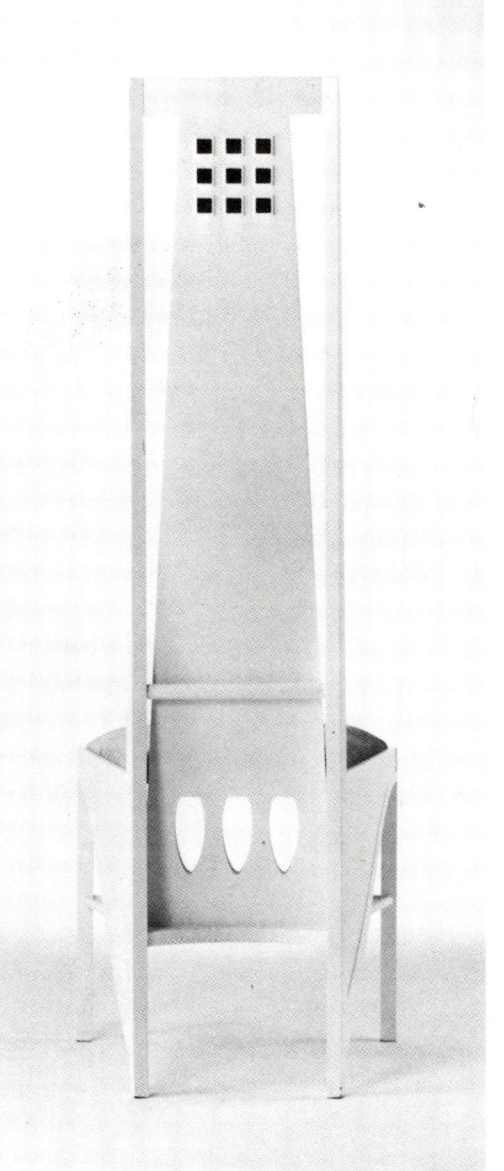

65

22 Curved Lattice Back Chair,
Willow Tearooms (1904)

Oak stained: 118,9 x 94 x 41 cm
(46¾ x 37 x 15¾ ins.)

Repr: *Dekorative Kunst,* VIII, 1905, p. 260 (original placing); Howarth, pl. 54 (original placing); GSA booklet, pl. 24; GSA F booklet, pl. 10; Macleod, p. 60.

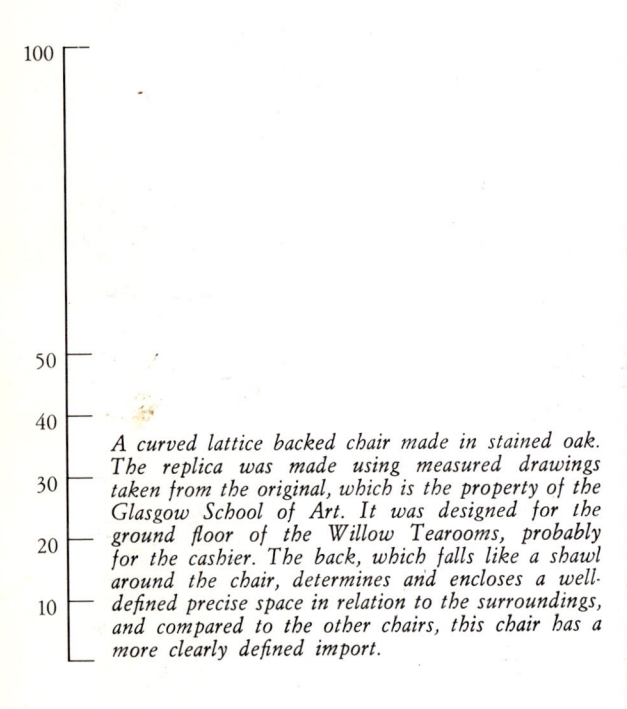

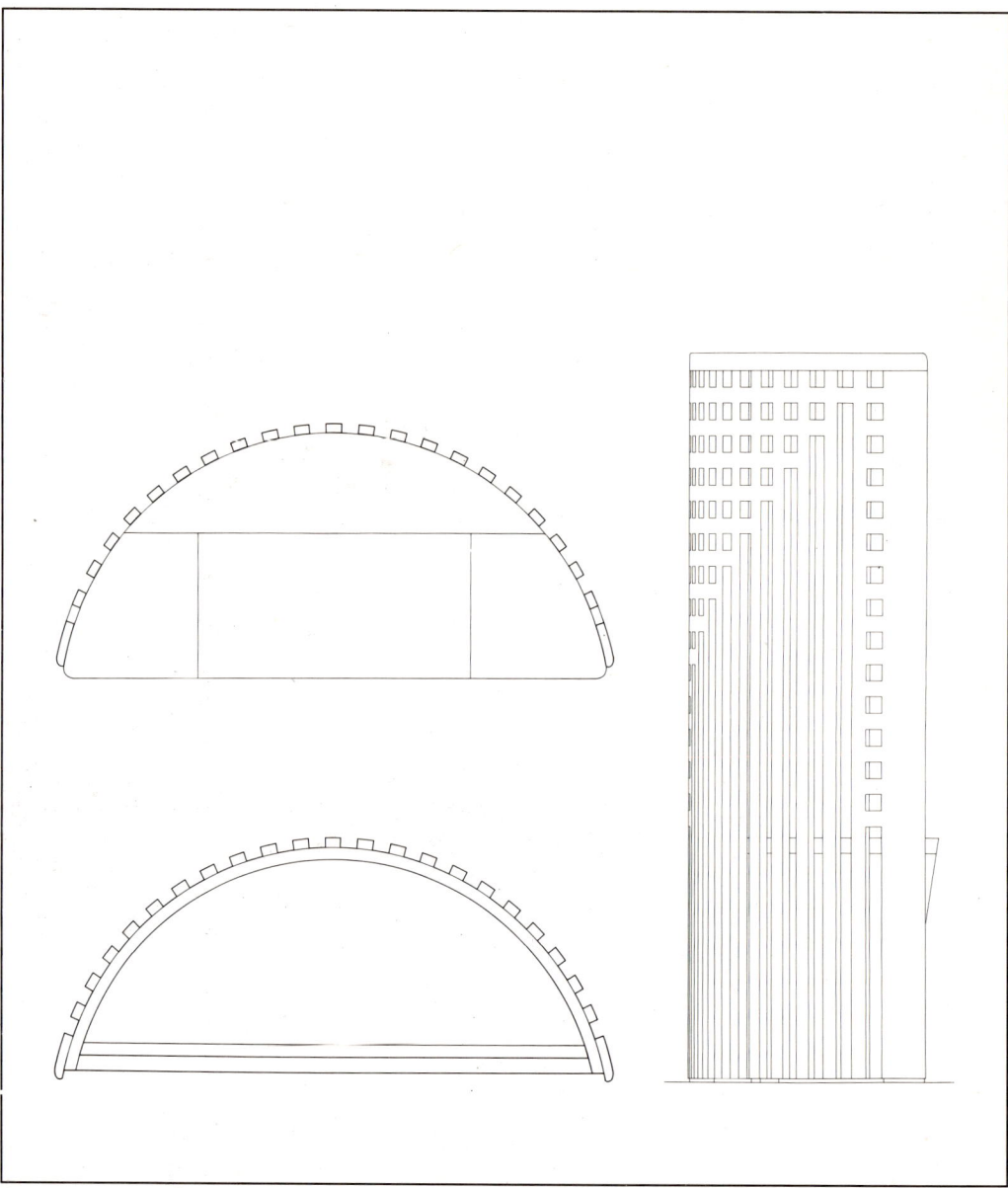

A curved lattice backed chair made in stained oak. The replica was made using measured drawings taken from the original, which is the property of the Glasgow School of Art. It was designed for the ground floor of the Willow Tearooms, probably for the cashier. The back, which falls like a shawl around the chair, determines and encloses a well-defined precise space in relation to the surroundings, and compared to the other chairs, this chair has a more clearly defined import.

66

SCHOOL OF THE MUSEUM
OF FINE ARTS · BOSTON

**23 Chair for Waitress,
Ingram Street Tearooms (1904)**

Oak, brown stain finish, seat upholstered:
63,5 x 45,5 x 45,5 cm (25 x 17⁷/₈ x 17⁷/₈ ins.)
Repr: GSA booklet, pl. 13.

A chair designed for a waitress, in stained oak with seat upholstered in material. The original was recovered from the Grosvenor restaurant in Glasgow and is now in the Glasgow School of Art. The orthogonal coordinates echo in attenuated form the spatial network of a little table inlaid with mother-of-pearl made for Hill House. In the table, the greater density of geometrical connections accentuates the division of space.

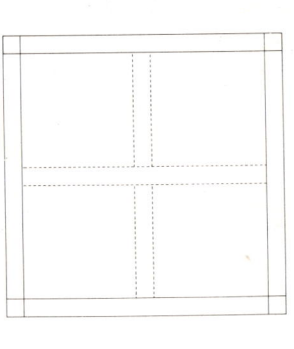

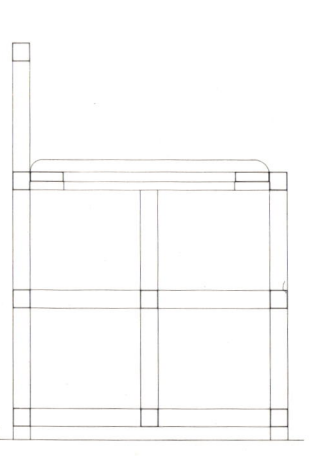

68

69

24 Chair with chequered vertical strips, Bedroom, Hous' Hill (1904)

Ebonized wood oak: 113,7 x 40,6 x 42 cm (43¾ x 16 x 16½ ins.)
Repr: Young, pl 26.

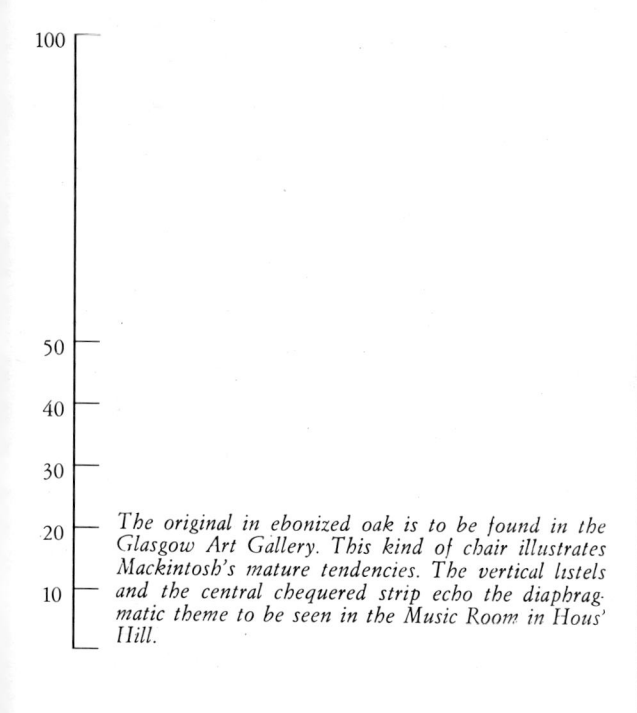

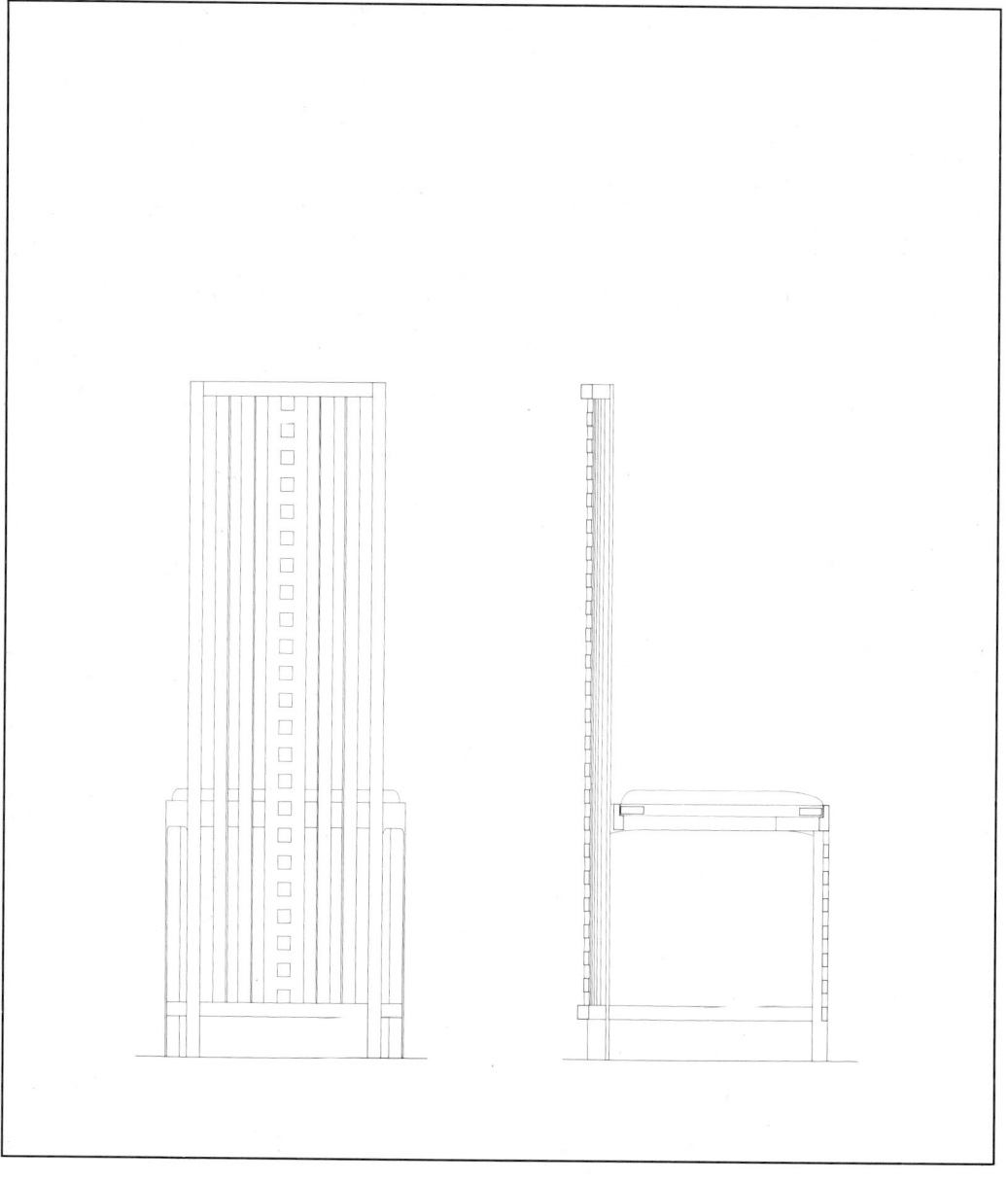

The original in ebonized oak is to be found in the Glasgow Art Gallery. This kind of chair illustrates Mackintosh's mature tendencies. The vertical listels and the central chequered strip echo the diaphragmatic theme to be seen in the Music Room in Hous' Hill.

71

SCHOOL OF THE MUSEUM
OF FINE ARTS · BOSTON

25/26 Chairs for Waitresses (1) and (2), from Ingram Street Tearooms (1907)

Oak ebonized, rush seating:
1   72,3 x 47 x 34,8 cm
    (28$^1/_2$ x 18$^1/_2$ x 13$^1/_2$ ins.)
2   74,5 x 41 x 35,2 cm
    (29$^1/_4$ x 16$^1/_8$ x 13$^3/_4$ ins.)
Repr: Macleod, p. 60; GSA F booklet, pl. 3.

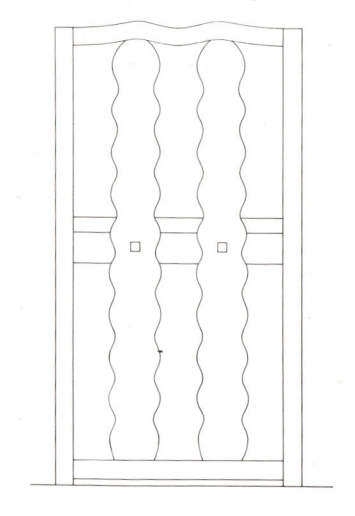

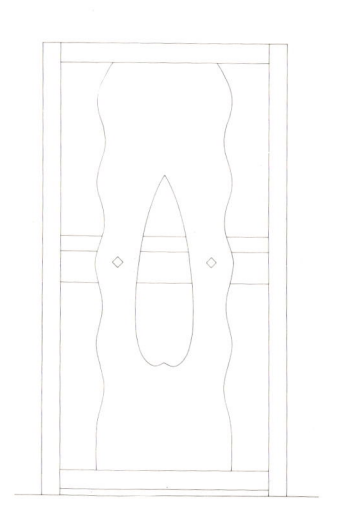

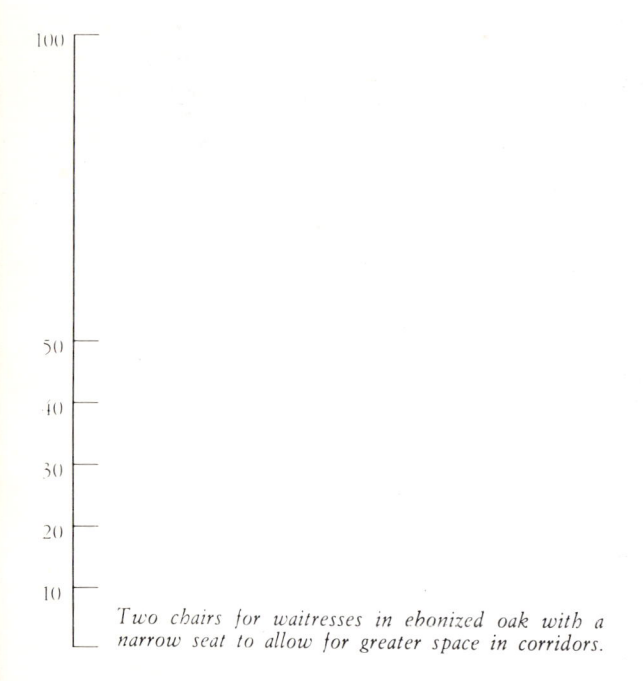

Two chairs for waitresses in ebonized oak with a narrow seat to allow for greater space in corridors.

73

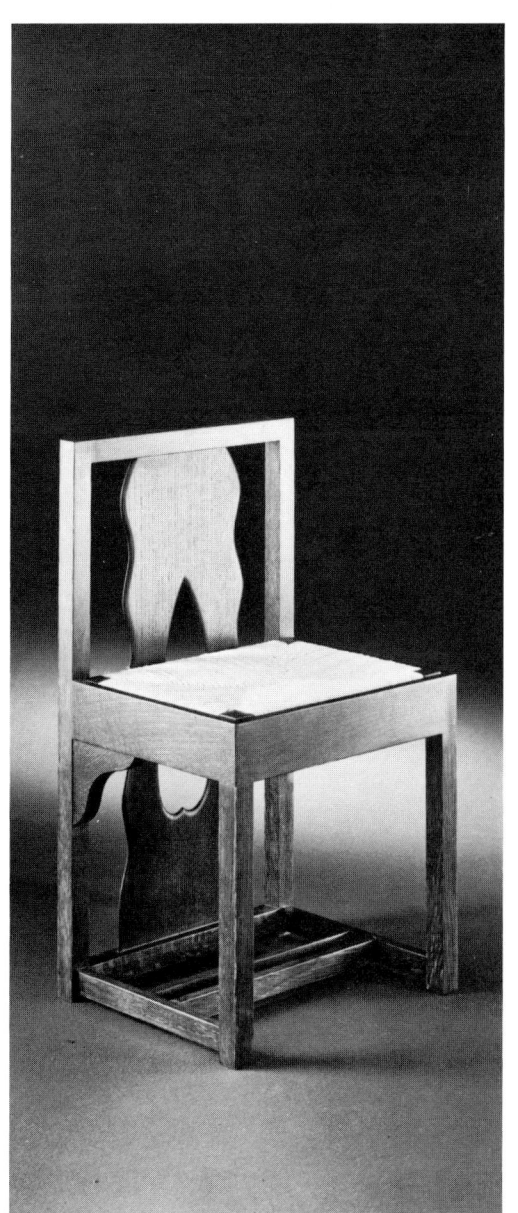

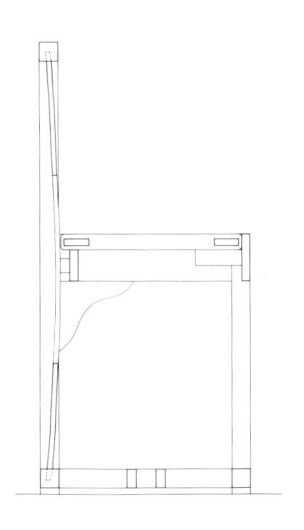

SCHOOL OF THE MUSEUM
OF FINE ARTS · BOSTON

27 **Chair with Low Fretwork Back,
for Ingram Street Tearooms (1910)**

Oak with seat upholstered:
83,2 x 43,5 x 40,3 cm (32½ x 17½ x 16 ins.)
Repr: GSA booklet, pl. 216; Macleod, p. 136.

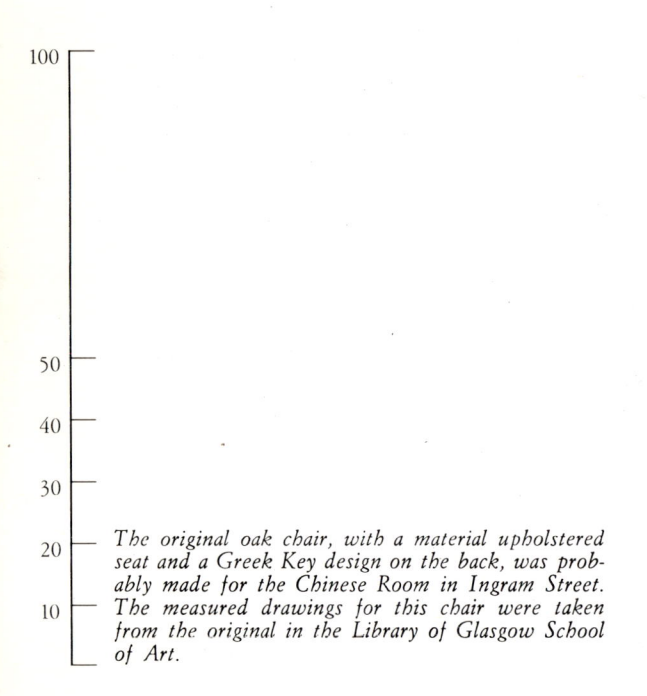

The original oak chair, with a material upholstered seat and a Greek Key design on the back, was probably made for the Chinese Room in Ingram Street. The measured drawings for this chair were taken from the original in the Library of Glasgow School of Art.

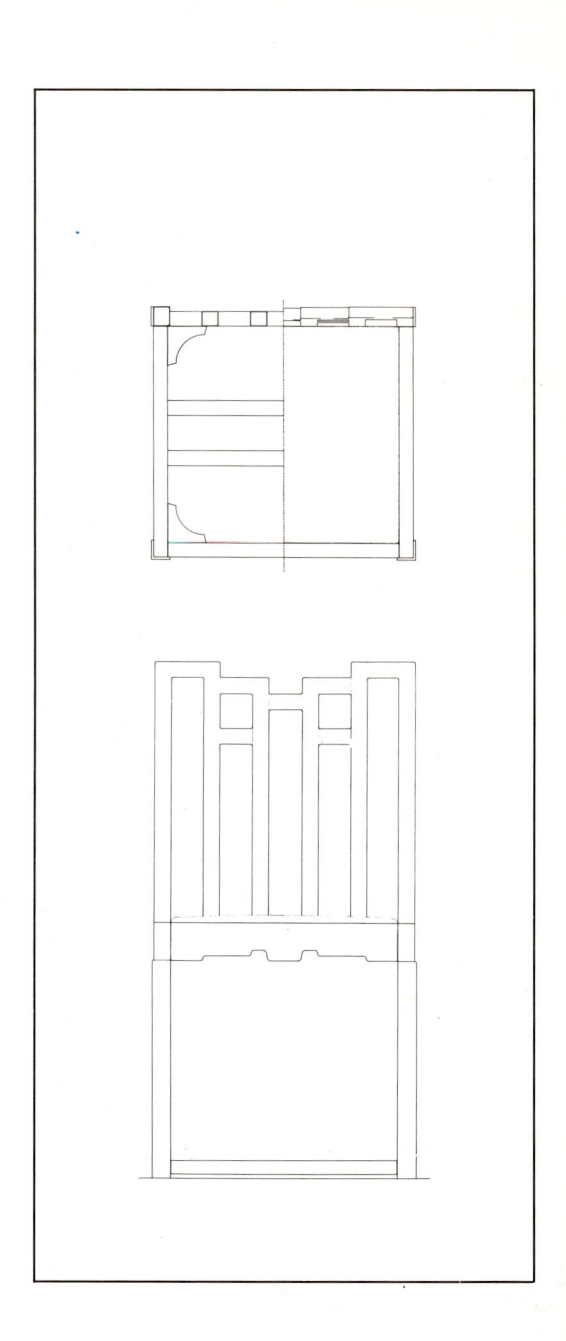

75

SCHOOL OF THE MUSEUM
OF FINE ARTS • BOSTON

76

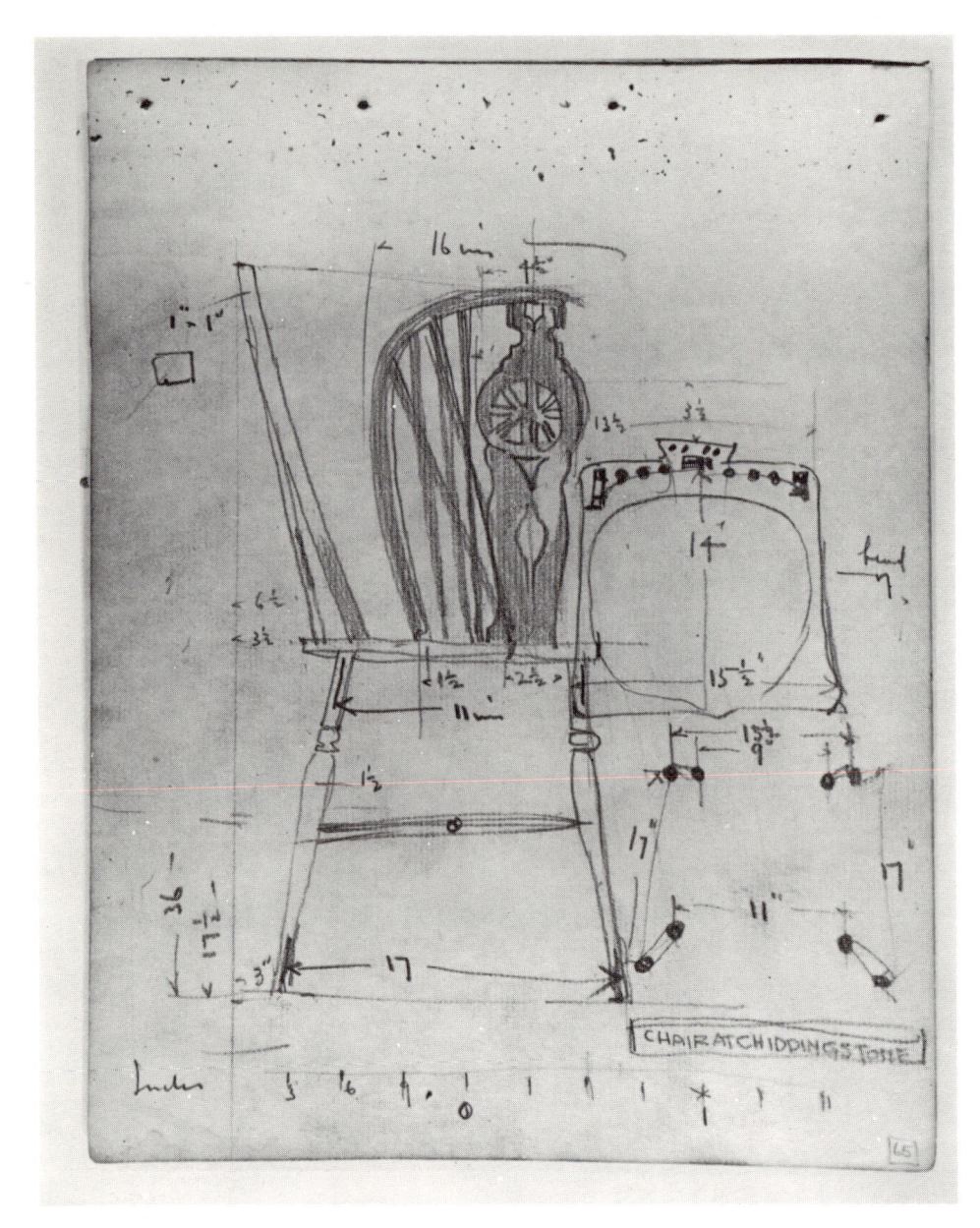

Chair at Chiddingstone, 1910.

Notes on Original Drawings

1
Design for chairs for smoking room,
Miss Cranston's Argyle Street Tearooms, Glasgow (1897-98)
Watercolour and pencil. 350×318 mm.

*The Argyle Street Tearooms, which belonged to Miss Catherine Cranston, were decorated and furnished by George Walton, another Glasgow architect and designer, and Mackintosh in 1897-98. Walton was responsible for the decorations and furnishings and Mackintosh for the moveable furniture.
Contemporary photographs show at least three of these chairs, made of stained oak, against the panelling in the Smoking Room.
(See Chair Nos. 1 and 2). G.U.*

2
Design for chairs and tables,
for Miss Cranston's Argyle Street Tearooms, Glasgow (1897-98)
Watercolour and pencil. 281×470 mm.

It is not known if these chairs were actually used in the Argyle Street Tearooms, as they do not appear in any contemporary photographs. Mackintosh, however, did use them in his own apartment. The drawing probably dates from the same period as No. 1, about 1897-98. (See Chair No. 3). G.U.

3
Design for a table and chair
for Miss Cranston (1897)
Watercolour and pencil. 210×325 mm.

Probably designed for the Argyle Street Tearooms. G.U.

4
Design for six pendant light fittings
for billiard room of Miss Cranston's
Argyle Street Tearooms, Glasgow (1897)
Watercolour and pencil. 453×240 mm.

The Glasgow Tearooms were far more than simple cafeterias or restaurants. They included Writing Room, Reading Room, Ladies Room, Smoking Rooms and usually Billiard Rooms for gentlemen visitors. G.U.

5
Designs for chairs
for Miss Cranston's Ingram Street Tearooms, Glasgow (1900)
Watercolour and pencil. 270×450 mm.

*These chairs with either a high back or a low back were used in the White Room of the Ingram Street Tearooms. Mackintosh kept some of the chairs for his own use, and painted one of the high chairs white, while leaving the others in the usual stained oak.
(See Chair Nos. 7, 8, 9). G.U.*

6
Design for furniture,
Hall of Windyhill, Kilmacolm (1900)
Watercolour and pencil. 319×705 mm.

*Mackintosh met William Davidson in the mid-1890's; he decorated and designed some furniture for the flat which Davidson occupied in his father's house Gladsmuir, at Kilmacolm.
In 1899 Davidson commissioned Mackintosh to design him a house, Windyhill at Kilmacolm. The table was certainly executed and appears in contemporary photographs of the hall; it now belongs to the Glasgow School of Art. The chairs, however, do not appear in any photographs of the hall; it is possible that they were rejected in favour of the chair with the tapering back, several of which were made for Windyhill about 1900 (see Drawing No. 7). G.U.*

7
Design for chair,
Windyhill, Kilmacolm (1900)
Watercolour and pencil. 266×323 mm.

A number of chairs of this design were made and they appear in contemporary photographs of the hall at Windyhill. They were made about 1900. (See Chair No. 10). G.U.

8
Design for a settle
Watercolour and pencil. 326×452 mm.

There is no indication of whether this settle was ever made, or for whom it was intended. It is a rather unusual piece of furniture, and another earlier drawing shows that Mackintosh was undecided about the height of the vertical section, and its depth. G.U.

9
Design for fireplace,
upper bedroom, Westdel, Glasgow (1900)
Watercolour and pencil. 236×428 mm.

*Mackintosh, by himself or on behalf of his firm, Honeyman and Keppie, took on a number of small commissions in or near Glasgow. In Westdel, which belonged to the Maclehose family, he designed a small bedroom and dressing room. All the fixed parts of this room, which probably dates from the same time as Windyhill, 1900, still remain, although the wall decoration is no longer visible.
This drawing shows the room more or less as it was executed; the next drawing shows an earlier stage of the design. G.U.*

10
Design for fireplace wall,
upper bedroom, Westdel, Glasgow (1900)
Watercolour and pencil. 318×500 mm. G.U.

11
Design for wall facing fireplace,
Westdel, Glasgow (1900)
Watercolour and pencil. 235×341 mm.

The decorative panels on the wardrobe that are shown in this drawing were altered in the final scheme, and that on the door to the dressing room was omitted entirely. G.U.

12
Design for window wall,
upper bedroom, Westdel, Glasgow (1900)
Watercolour and pencil. 235×341 mm. G.U.

13
Two square silver-plated lamps
with coloured leaded glass insets
and circular tops (1900)

These lamps were designed for Mackintosh's own flat in Mains Street, Glasgow. There they used gas, but when Mackintosh moved to a larger house in

78 *Autumn*, 1894.

Southpark Avenue they served just as well for electricity. Probably made about 1900. G.U.

14
Two embroidered panels
Embroidery and applique on linen.
1822 × 496 mm.

These two panels were designed for the principal bedroom at Hill House and appear in Mackintosh's drawings of the east wall of the bedroom. It is not known whether they were installed at Hill House, for the early photographs taken in 1904 do not show them, although the panels themselves were reproduced in « Deutsche Kunst und Dekoration » in 1902.
Walter Blackie, who commissioned Hill House, certainly received them from Margaret for it was he who presented them to the School of Art. G.S.A.

15
Fish knife and fork
Silver plated nickel. 230 mm.

Probably dating from 1903 or after. G.U.

16
Cutlery from the Ingram Street Tearooms, Glasgow
(a) *Soup spoon: silver plated nickel. 184 mm.*
(b) *Dinner knife and fork: steel and silver plated nickel with composition handles. 265 and 210 mm.*
(c) *Tea knife: steel and silver plated nickel with composition handle. 226 mm.*
(d) *Tea spoon: silver plated nickel. 153 mm.*

They were all probably designed about 1903. G.S.A.

17
Design for a writing cabinet,
Hill House, Helensburgh (1903-4)
Watercolour and pencil. 310 × 398 mm.

Hill House at Helensburgh was designed by Mackintosh in 1902 for Walter Blackie, the publisher. Mackintosh was concerned with every feature of the house, and it is still substantially as he left it. Mackintosh remained a friend of the Blackie family and in subsequent visits to the house he would occasionally be asked to design new furniture for it, as in the case of this writing cabinet. The silver panel on the interior also appears in a desk designed for Michael Diack.
(See also page 58). G.U.

18
Designs for writing cabinet and chair,
Hill House, Helensburgh (1904)
Watercolour and pencil. 265 × 460 mm.

Another design, marked No. 2, also exists, but does not include the chair.
(See Chair No. 24). G.U.

19
Plan of principal bedroom, Hill House,
showing position of the furniture and sketch
of an easy chair (1903-4)
Watercolour and pencil. 330 × 538 mm.

Hill House was planned with immense detail, and Mackintosh even decided the exact position of such loose furniture as chairs and tables. Most of the furniture still remains in the room. G.U.

20
Design for wall decoration and furniture,
principal bedroom, Hill House, south wall (1903-4)
Watercolour and pencil. 347 × 647 mm.

The finished room varied slightly from the drawing: the table was of a different design, the central post was omitted, the decoration either side of the post was used instead of the roses on the right of the drawing, and the seat beneath the bay window was omitted.
(See Chair No. 18). G.U.

21
Design for a lampshade,
Hill House, Helensburgh (1904)
Watercolour and pencil. 600 × 699 mm.

This drawing for a very ornate lampshade may well have been made after Hill House was completed. The decoration on it is similar to that used in the Principal Bedroom, particularly on the washstand. It was intended to be made of silk, a sample of which is attached to the drawing, with ribbon and embroidered decoration. G.U.

22
Drawings for chairs,
Hous'Hill (1904)
Watercolour and pencil. 325 × 425 mm.

John Cochrane was the husband of Catherine Cranston, who had commissioned the Tearoom interiors from Mackintosh. At their home, Hous' Hill, Mackintosh remodelled the interiors, but discreetly accommodated their antique furniture alongside his own.
These chairs were used in the Music Room, and were made of stained or ebonized wood, with coloured glass inlays. G.U.

23
Drawings for bedroom furniture,
Hous'Hill (1904)
Watercolour and pencil. 350 × 870 mm.

Hous' Hill was demolished in 1933 and few of the items designed by Mackintosh still exist. A small bedroom chair, of stained sycamore, now belongs to Glasgow University; it is similar to the small chair shown in this drawing, but it is narrower and does not have the same curved back.
A contemporary photograph shows this chair at the foot of the bed, as it is in the drawing, so Mackintosh must again have changed the design. The drawing probably dates from late 1904. (See Chair No. 19). G.U.

24
Designs for two chairs and a cabinet
Pencil and wash. 248 × 422 mm.

It is not known if either the chairs or the cabinet shown in this drawing were ever made. The chairs are more ornate than most other chairs designed by Mackintosh. The motif of the rose with falling petals seen twice on the cabinet, was also used by Mackintosh on a desk designed for Michael Diack. G.U.

25
Design for a lampshade,
Hill House, Helensburgh (1904)
Watercolour and pencil. 558 × 401 mm.

This shade is very similar to the one designed for Hous' Hill, although the design is more rectilinear, as was the furniture at Hill House. G.U.

26
Design for a chair and table
for an Austrian or German client (1903-4)
Watercolour and pencil. 256 × 470 mm.

As this drawing is inscribed with the names of the objects in German, and it bears Mackintosh's private address, not that of his office, it is likely that this was a private commission from an Austrian or German client. The furniture has never been traced, but what is interesting is that the furniture is almost identical to that designed for the Room de Luxe of the Willow Tearooms, Glasgow, in 1903-4. G.U.

27
Design for interior decoration and chairs
for an Austrian or German client (1904)
Watercolour and pencil. 332 × 513 mm.

This drawing is probably for the same scheme as Nos. 26, 28, 29, 30, but neither the client nor the furniture has ever been traced. G.U.

28
Design for bedroom furniture and decoration
for an Austrian or German client (1904)
Watercolour and pencil. 350 × 505 mm. G.U.

29
Design for bedroom furniture
for an Austrian or German client (1904)
Watercolour and pencil. 330 × 410 mm. G.U.

30
Design for bedroom furniture
for an Austrian of German client (1904)
Watercolour and pencil. 350 × 495 mm. G.U.

31
Designs for chairs and tables,
Ladies' Room of Miss Cranston's Willow Tearooms,
Sauchiehall Street, Glasgow (1903-4)
Watercolour and pencil. 323 × 520 mm.

The other chairs and tables in this room, usually known as the Room de Luxe, were similar to those shown in drawing No. 26. The Room de Luxe (and the furniture and fittings in it) was one of the finest rooms which Mackintosh created for Miss Cranston. Unfortunately the chairs and tables have disappeared from the room, which is otherwise well preserved. Examples of both

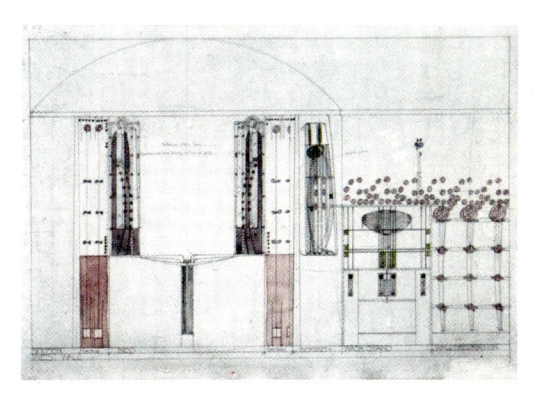

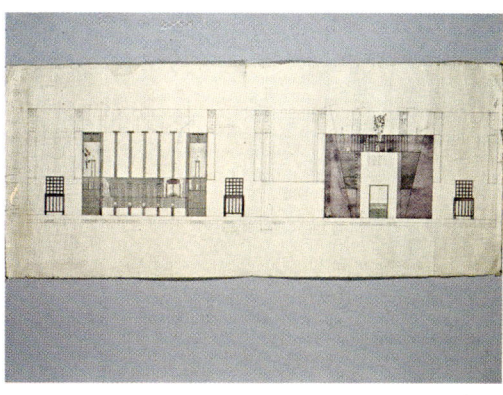

Hill House, Helensburgh, 1903, bedroom wall and wall decoration.
Hous'Hill, 1905, bedroom wall.

the high and low backed chairs have recently been discovered, and one of each is now in the Glasgow University Collection. G.U.

32
Design for chairs and tables,
Back Saloon of Miss Cranston's Willow Tearooms,
Sauchiehall Street, Glasgow (1903-4)
Watercolour and pencil. 346×488 mm.

Like drawing No. 31, this was probably done in 1903-4. G.U.

33
Soup spoon, meat fork, dessert spoon and fork
Silver. Soup spoon, 266 mm; meat fork, 260 mm; dessert spoon and fork, 235 mm.

Probably from 1906. M.N.S.

34
Design for light fittings on ground and first floors,
Glasgow School of Art (1907-9)
Watercolour and pencil. 317×257 mm.

These were types of lamp intended for the Library in the Glasgow School of Art, and they were designed in 1907-9. The lamp shown here is the smaller version, which was hung singly in the gallery, and underneath it. Its light was directed downwards on to the tables beneath, with very little light escaping through the shade itself. G.U.

35
Design for central pendant light fitting
in the Library, Glasgow School of Art (1907-9)
Watercolour and pencil. 360×224 mm.

Three different lamp shades were grouped together, at different heights, to form a central pendant fitting for the new Library. Each of the three designs is a variation of the lamps used in the gallery, and they are made of sheet steel out of which the design is stamped. Designed about 1907-9, their angularity repeats in reduced scale that of the Library itself. G.U.

36
Flower drawing - Spurge (1909)
Watercolour and pencil. 258×203 mm.
G.U.

Textile and fabric designs, 1916-20.

37
Margaret Macdonald Mackintosh:
Menu for The White Cockade
Colour lithograph. 216 × 318 mm.

The White Cockade was a temporary café designed for Miss Cranston for the Glasgow International Exhibition of 1911. The original design for this menu is in the Glasgow University Collection. G.S.A.

38
Flower drawing - Larkspur (1914)
Watercolour and pencil. 258 × 203 mm.

After Mackintosh left Glasgow in 1914 he went to stay in Walberswick, where he made a number of such flower studies. Some authorities have interpreted the joint signature of Mackintosh and his wife as meaning that Mackintosh did the drawing and Margaret the colouring. It is unlikely that Mackintosh would have allowed this and as further refutation, another flower drawing has five initials on it: a more likely interpretation is that the initials record the people present when the drawing was made. G.U.

39
Flower drawing - Japanese Witch Hazel (1915)
Watercolour and pencil on paper. 260 × 210 mm. G.U.

40
Flower drawing - Fritillaria (1915)
Watercolour and pencil. 251 × 202 mm. G.U.

41
Gorse, Walberswick (1915)
Watercolour and pencil. 260 × 204 mm. H.J.B.

42
Anemone and Pasque, Walberswick (1915)
Watercolour and pencil. 260 × 204 mm. H.J.B.

43
Scale drawing for cupboard for coats in Hall, Derngate, Northampton (1915)
Watercolour and pencil. 298 × 399 mm.

About 1915 W.J. Bassett-Lowke, of the Northampton engineering and model-making firm, was put in touch with Mackintosh who was, by this time, settled in Chelsea. Mackintosh designed a bedroom for him in

Margaret Macdonald: fabric design, 1916-20.

82 *Leaves*, 1909.

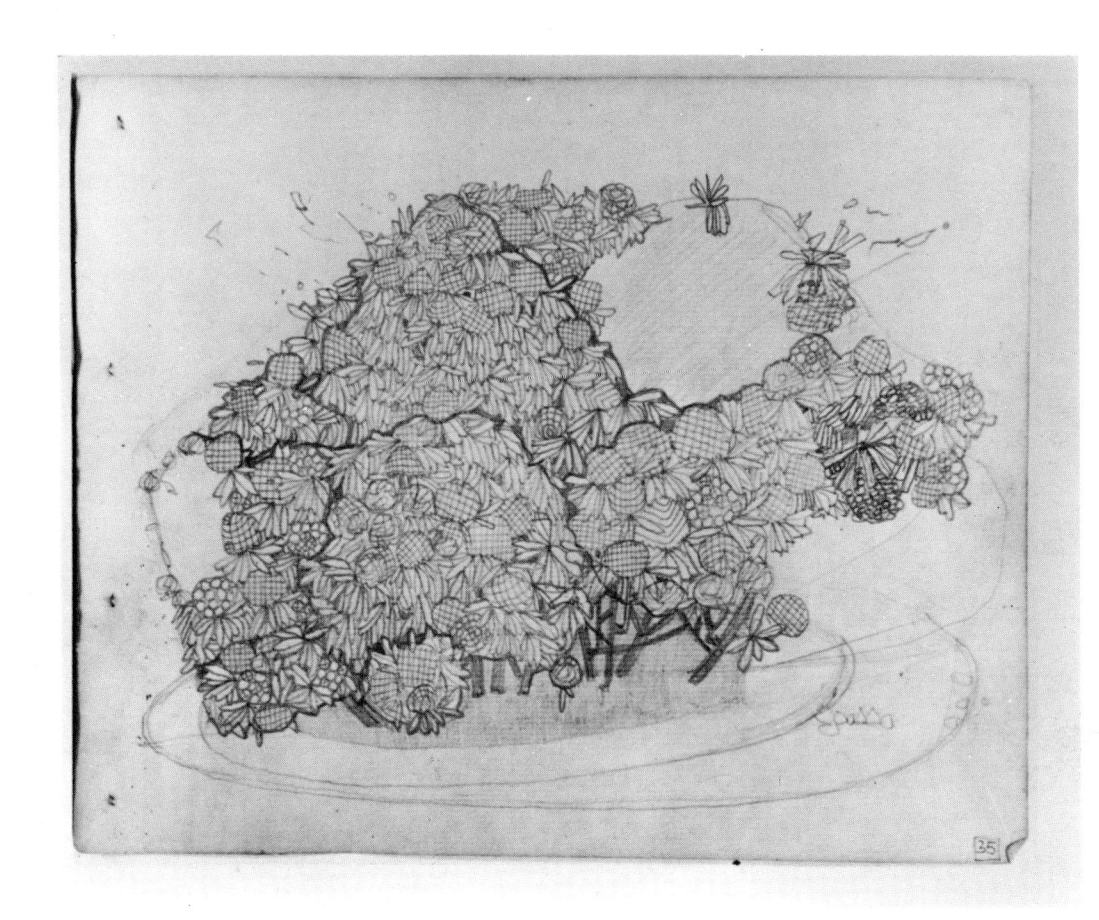

his parents' house. This met with approval and was followed by an invitation to design a room for Bassett-Lowke's friend, F. Jones. When in 1916 Bassett-Lowke and his wife moved to their first home in a terraced house at 78 Derngate, Mackintosh had remodelled and refurnished it completely. He was also later to design furniture for the Bassett-Lowke's weekend cottage, Candida Cottage.
In his Northampton work Mackintosh developed the angularity which began to appear in his later decorative work in Glasgow - most markedly in the Cloister Room of the Ingram Street Tearooms for Miss Cranston. The front door, screen and fireplace of Derngate were all executed much as they appear in the drawings: the wall decoration, however, became more elaborate. G.U.

44
Scale drawing of staircase screen in Hall, Derngate, Northampton (1918)
Watercolour and pencil. 343 × 516 *mm. G.U.*

45
Fabric design (1916-20)
Watercolour and ink. 255 × 255 *mm.*

From about 1916 until the early 1920's Mackintosh produced a vast number of fabric designs, some of which were accepted by the London textile firms, Foxton's and Sefton's. Usually, they are a formalization of natural forms, but in some cases this formalization is taken to the extreme of total abstraction. G.U.

46
Textile design (1916-20)
Watercolour and pencil. 397 × 288 *mm. G.U.*

47
Textile design (furniture fabric) (1916-20)
Watercolour and pencil on brown tracing paper laid on white tracing paper. 298 × 217 *mm.*

The vertical bands and waves of this abstract design barely suggest the natural forms on which it is based. G.U.

48
Textile design (1916-20)
Watercolour and pencil on brown tracing paper. 400 × 393 *mm. G.U.*

The Dover House, Chiddingstone, 1910.

49
Textile design (1916-20)
*Watercolour and pencil on brown tracing paper.
262 × 210 mm. G.U.*

50
Textile design
*Watercolour and pencil. 240 × 190 mm.
H.J.B.*

51
Textile design
Watercolour and pencil. 310 × 190 mm.

*This drawing shows the three colour ways of No. 50.
H.J.B.*

52
Textile design
Watercolour and pencil. 240 × 194 mm. H.J.B.

53
North wall, Rest Room, Willow Tearooms (1917)
Watercolour and pencil. 290 × 752 mm. G.S.A.

54
West wall. Rest Room, Willow Tearooms (1917)
Watercolour and pencil. 368 × 715 mm.

*Miss Cranston extended the Willow Tearooms by
opening a room in the basement called
"The Dugout". These drawings would seem to be
related to this scheme, the predominant colour
of which was black.
The settle shown in the drawing of the north
walls is now in the collection of the Glasgow
School of Art. G.S.A.*

55
Drawing of sideboard, table and one chair
for W.T. Bassett-Lowke Esq. (1918)
Watercolour and pencil. 364 × 782 mm. G.U.

56
Scale drawings for dining room furniture,
table chairs and coffee table (1918)
Watercolour and pencil. 317 × 785 mm. G.U.

57
Three Chelsea Studios, elevation to Glebe Place
(1920)
*Watercolour and pencil on light brown paper.
276 × 372 mm. H.J.B.*

58
Three Chelsea Studios, elevation to Cheyne House Garden (1920)
Watercolour and pencil on light brown paper. 276×372 mm.

In 1920 Mackintosh was commissioned to design studios for three artists, Harold Squire, Derwent Wood and A. Blunt on a site between Glebe Place and Cheyne House Row. Adjoining them was to be a block of studios for the Arts League of Service.
Only the studio for Harold Squire was ever built, and even this was substantially modified.
In his diary for 1920 Mackintosh accounts for the time spent on the drawing for the artists' studios and the completed plans were submitted to the planning authority. There is no indication of why the scheme was dropped; perhaps it was the disapproval of the London Council, or the high cost of the scheme. H.J.B.

59
Studio Block for the Arts League of Service (1920)
Watercolour and pencil on light brown paper. 276×372 mm.

This block, together with another in Glebe Place, was to provide studio-flats for artists and architects, who had formed a cooperative association, the Arts League of Service. A site was chosen adjacent to that for Harold Squire's house, previously occupied by old Cheyne House, Chelsea. Mackintosh's plans were at first rejected by the authorities, described as factory-like and "not architectural enough". There were not enough ornaments, swags or pediments for the officials, but eventually Mackintosh received permission to go ahead on December 19, 1920. Again, the scheme was never carried out, probably because funds could not be raised for what appears to have been an expensive building. H.J.B.

60
Facsimile of wall decoration at Derngate, Northampton

This shows Mackintosh's original design for the decoration of the hall of Derngate: all the patterning was based on triangles and squares, and the unpatterned walls, floors and ceilings were painted black. This predominantly black scheme of decoration was overpowering to the Bassett-Lowkes and Mackintosh replaced it, after about a year, with one consisting of groups of overlapping triangles placed on a light ground. This second scheme so pleased them that when, in 1925, they moved to New Ways, the house designed for them by Peter Behrens, the same stencils were used for the decoration of the study. G.U.

61
The Downs, Worth Matavers
Watercolour. 442 × 530 mm.

Mackintosh visited Dorset in July of 1920 and painted many watercolours around Worth Matavers. G.S.A.

62
Flower study, Mont Louis (1925)
Watercolour and pencil. 260 × 204 mm. H.J.B.

63
Le Fort Maillert (1927)
Watercolour. 345×265 mm.

Mackintosh left London in 1923, and settled in the South of France, first at Mont Louis in the Pyrenées, and later at Port Vendres, on the Mediterranean side of the Franco-Spanish border. He had given up architecture altogether and now spent his time making watercolours. In all of them, however, there is a strong formal content. This fort is also reminiscent, in its site and construction, of the castle at Holy Island which Mackintosh knew well, and had drawn in 1901. G.S.A.

Lenders
G.U. University of Glasgow, Mackintosh Collection
G.S.A. Glasgow School of Art Collection
H.J.B. Collection of Mr. and Mrs. H. Jefferson Barnes, Lochghilphead, Argyle
M.N.S. Collection of Mrs. Mary Newbery Sturrock, Edinburgh

Port Vendres, 1923-27.

SCHOOL OF THE MUSEUM
OF FINE ARTS · BOSTON

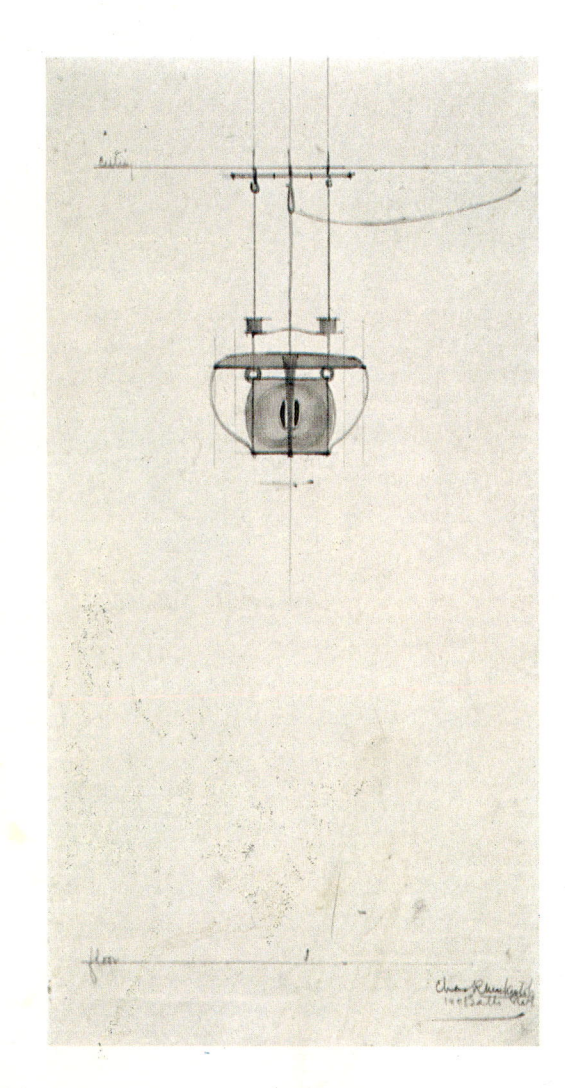

86　*Light fitting, Argyle Street Tearooms, 1897.*

Critical Analysis of the Chairs

1/2
Low and High Back Armchair, (tub-chair) for Smoking Room, Argyle Street Tearooms (1897)

This is the first chair we have studied in the series of chairs designed by Mackintosh. It was presented to the public in the Smoking Room of the Argyle Street Tearooms around 1897, when contemporary furniture frequently consisted of traditionally robust reproductions, or alternatively belonged to that contemporary school of thought, the Arts and Crafts Movement.

This is an armchair which sums up Mackintosh's ideological patrimony; a patrimony which he himself had described some years previously (February, 1891) when he read a paper, « Scottish Baronial Architecture », to the Glasgow Architectural Association. After he had made a theoretical requalification of indigenous style, and criticised a Greek and Roman revival which had so noticeably dominated all the architecture of the country, Mackintosh inspired materials with a creative spirit and thus produced valuable examples of "applied art".

The artist's predilection for geometrical patterns is displayed in the fundamentally cubic plan of the chair, a plan which expresses itself in the total structure. The artist's recourse to the shapes of elementary geometrical solids denotes his desire to express himself unequivocally in a language which does not lend itself to superficial interpretations, and can only be understood in terms of rigorous parallel with his theoretical premises.

This chair, so elegant in its essentiality, symmetry and confluence, is a homage to the austere simplicity of the Scottish vernacular, and thus to Mackintosh's remarkable touch, by that time already exercised and educated. It is not difficult to explain why the vernacular style pleased and aroused consensus and admiration. Mackintosh depended on just that "principle of absorption" which results in the style or shape of an object, becoming diffuse and desirable, while mediating that process of sedimentation of archetypal forms which in time, juxtaposed and combined, qualify a matrix common to the object and to its environment. « *The indigenous tradition which has been the architecture of that same country of ours is not less Scottish than we ourselves are, nor less indigenous than our countryside, the wild flowers in our fields, our famous forbears, our traditions and our political institutions.* » The monastic and medieval austerity of the Scottish line, tempered by the artist's grace (Mackintosh had purified his intellectual spirit studying the masterpieces of Italian architecture), is an element to be found in any analytical study of any of Mackintosh's productions.

Now, if the theoretical physiognomy of our chair is a closed elaborate solid cube, which has the intention of producing a functional and visually pleasing object, its material realisation (a structure of fitted planes and confluences on a single axis) reveals two factors which are characteristic and constant in all the artist's constructive works. One factor is the study of techniques and the relative attempt, in the actual phase of construction, to remain faithful, as far as was possible, to the original figuration in order to translate it into reality with integrity. The other factor is no less interesting an artistic attribute, faithfulness to the ultimate aim and function of the object. In the practical development of a chair, every detail in fact combines to form and individualize a well-calibrated volume which succeeds in making it a welcoming womb.

It is not, therefore, important that the chair is affiliated to another chair with a high horizontally-banded back. What is important is the primitive concept of concretizing the seating function in a perfect, closed, geometrical solid. Hence the necessity of relying on surfaces, more than on uprights, for the function of delimiting the object, basing the structural criterion of the construction on the presence of visible axes as the fundamental elements, whilst the surface outlines perform the function of ultimate connection and determination of the solid form of the object. The joining of these surfaces, the walls of the chair therefore, constitute the Archimedic node of structure, particularly as that connection of the surfaces is identified with the supporting pillars.

It is worth remembering that, if ever a detailed analysis of the functional structure may become barren, the value of the object lies solely in its ultimate composition, a composition which is the daily research of the artist in his eidetic attitude vis-à-vis art. The mouldings and the curves present in this chair are a part of the already complete patrimony of the designer. The lateral face of the chair presents at the bottom a curve which wells up from the rear foot, growing as it rises towards the front upright, whilst at the top the same descending matrix flows into the joining of the arm. The composition of curved lines is the only valid method of expressing and visualizing not only a cer-

Armchair for Smoking Room, Argyle Street Tearooms, 1897.

88 *Lug chair, Mains Street flat,* 1901.

tain dynamism in the leaning area, but also that sense of stability necessary to the user of the chair. It is worthwhile repeating, to avoid eventual misunderstanding, that this language is a peculiar gift of Mackintosh, and is a language whose rules he continued to develop and perfect.

In a later chair we will see an ascending motif returning in an essential support function, even if the curve surface relationship becomes modified. Referring once more to this beautiful little chair, the different lines of the lower and upper curves, especially the former, accentuate an impression of greater stability and of gravitation of weight onto the rear feet. The upper curve, to which is entrusted the function of bestowing and visualizing the quality of being suitable for leaning against, develops with sinuous movement, starting with a line orthogonal to the rear pillar. It also functions as a tensional pull between front and rear pillars in order to end in relation to the armrest which in turn leans upon it. Finally, the linking of the two pillars and the necessity of strengthening the support find a solution in the simultaneous perception of two joint curves, whilst the intensive dynamism of the composition results in a diminution of that sense of grossness which inevitably accompanies such extensive surfaces as one observes from the side view. The observer imagining himself about to sit, thinks of himself as slipping towards the back, perceiving an illusory slope; but in reality the pillars are exactly level and the seat is perfectly horizontal.

One must agree that Mackintosh respected the relationship between the object as a concept, and the object as a reality. The chair is entirely of solid wood, eliminating upholstery which would, in this case, be irrelevant to the structure, and thus he avoids any other form overlapping the original matrix; however, he shapes the form of the buttocks on the seat.

The solution is certainly within the canons of the Scottish vernacular, and is faithful to the dictates of the Arts and Crafts Movement.

To complete the analysis, it is essential to consider briefly the significance and presence of the arcs on the front and back views. It has already been said that once Mackintosh achieved an intuitive feeling for the exact significance and innate value of a given curve, he was able to develop and perfect it into a notable characteristic of his work. Here he prefers to use a low arc because he has discovered that, compared to the stability and rigidity of the high arc, the low arc creates tension and dynamism because of the force which it seems to have to resist. Once he isolated this phenomenon as a way of projecting horizontal tension, and of connecting uprights, Mackintosh develops this theme, continually qualifying its precise formal value to the point of using it as an illusory and synthetic expression for symbolic drapery.

3
**Chair with Oval Backrail,
Argyle Street Tearooms (1897)**

At first glance the 1897 chair appears to speak of a designer who was far from being indifferent to the Art and Crafts Movement. Just at that time, in fact, William Morris (1889) was expounding his point of view on the necessity of re-discovering the spirit and the craftmanship of English artists in the later medieval period.

« ... *Twofold is the aim of setting art to utilitarian objects, first of all to add beauty to the result of human work, which otherwise could be ugly; secondly, to give delight to the very work, which else would be unpleasant and disgusting...* » (1)

Morris also suggested that the intrinsic quality of a material be considered important in itself, without recourse to the artifice which attempted to pass as marble a plaster wall painted to look like marble.

In this chair, as in all the chairs made before 1900, the oak is deliberately left unpainted, and is exposed in all its essentiality, in order to re-acquire the correspondence between expression and function.

Respect for tradition and for the Scottish vernacular found full realisation here without obscuring that other typical aspect of the Arts and Crafts Movement, namely creating an individuality for a piece of furniture which could distinguish it from an industrially produced piece.

Mackintosh never indulges in the repetition of information already expressed, not even in minute particulars such as the carving of the fringe of the wooden balustrades in the Library, nor in the carving on the top of the legs of a series of tables from that same Library in the Glasgow School of Art. Each chair is unique even if all together they form part of a singular series.

If one carefully examines the sketches of interiors and furnishings which he usually prepared before actual construction, one can understand that in the creative moment, Mackintosh had conceived an interior design in its two-dimensional form. In the chair we are studying here, the distinctive artistic merit of the piece is to be found in the

(1) William Morris, « Architecture and Socialism », quoted from memory.

fundamental equilibrium of the form, and in the manner in which it is projected from whatever point of observation one takes. The back view looks like a tall picture delimited by two lateral uprights and by the top and bottom cross-bars. Alternatively one can view it in terms of the two long bands which express in neo-Gothic semantic the dynamic ascensional osmosis between the material of which the chair is made and the aesthetic quality of the configuration, that dynamic configuration between the lower horizontal and the noble conclusion that is the top. Only the perceptual organization of the observer gives unity to this astonishing pattern, and this happens because Mackintosh treats space with quite remarkable effects. Analysis of this effect emphasises the rôle of the two bands which initially determine an area, and delimit and substantiate its gently tapering upward movement.

Even though it echoes previous attempts at a synthesis of medieval and renaissance artisan connotations, for example the chair for the smoking room, here we see the achievement of an artistic goal after long debate with contemporary thinkers on the comparative rôle of function and beauty.

A new element in Mackintosh's artistic physiognomy is the assumption, now always present, of the decorative function of structure. If one considers that the idea of the decorative function of structure was at this time a concept of the future, the work of Mackintosh is seen to be quite novel, and different from previous and contemporary interior design. One is aware of the ascensional emphasis given to a vertical composition by the acute tense arc of the crossbar. This curve, rather than any whimsical decoration, gives a new merit to the ascending perspective of the central bands. It

Birds, 1893-94.

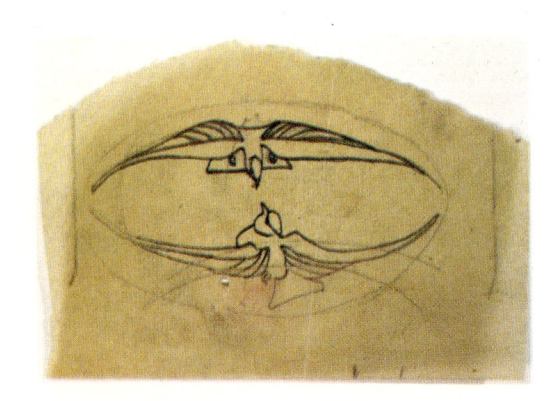

bestows a substantial equilibrium on the lateral pillars and at the same time qualifies the pseudo-ellipse of the summit which in profile, liberated from any heterogeneous preoccupation, is freed from pomposity, and establishes a nodal point for the observer. Until the end of the last century, the upper part of a building, or of an item of furniture, was designed to agree significantly with the style of the whole, and at the same time served as a dividing element in surrounding space and in any two-dimensional representation of the object, thus increasing the two-dimensionality.

Mackintosh cultivated tradition, and yet was a researcher into, and innovator of, new form; his interior universe contained a figurative synthesis of pure and perfect lines, primary volumes and surfaces. He loved the quiet of the cylinder, the cube and the sphere, and resolved here, in a simple concave ellipse, that need to distribute iconography, structure and function. There is no doubt that because of its dimension, proportion and form, the top of this chair constitutes a unity in itself. As such it fulfills perfectly its function as a screen, and as a background for the head of the person who sits on it.

The characteristic message given by this element of the chair is the separate statement made by its perimetral line and the concavity of its surface; and it is thus not a mass which interrupts surrounding empty space, but a concave container of space where the atmosphere seems to accumulate. Here in short, Mackintosh has managed to create a sort of body, indeed a cushion born up by that same air which appears to be concentrated at this point.

A final proof for our interpretation is offered to us in the moon-shaped carving which rides in the middle of the piece in question. It is not so much the carving that is striking, as the relationship of the carving to the whole. The shape chosen is the end product of lengthy study (it appeared before this in a calendar, designed by him, where similar forms are joined to each other). The idea is the culmination of several refinements in this pure figure which is perfectly integrated with the perimeter of the ellipse, and which serves to solder together, figuratively, the central band with the ellipse itself, almost as though the bands extended ideally beyond the point in order to disperse. Basically the figure is composed of an arc of a circle overhung by another arc, and attached in the centre to a slight counter-curve. A less minute interpretation of the design suggests two lateral horns spread out in isolation like flapping wings attached to a central body. Because of the convexity of the surface this appears more voluminous from the back. Perhaps in comparing various interpretations of this element of the chair one loses semantic precision, but one gains a powerful sensation of movement, and a tension that transcends any static quality, animates and enriches the imagination creating the impression of a body in flight. Because this figure is the end-result of a long period of archetypal sedimentation, it assumes the function of a very real symbol in the design patrimony of Mackintosh, and appears later in other chairs and on the swing doors of the School of Art.

Although the summit of the chair may appear isolated, it can be seen that it shares in the communication of the whole, in the reciprocal influence of one part upon another, the lower curve with the curve of the top, the bands with the slight concavity, together showing a fundamental unity.

From the side view the observers' interest is taken in a way which lends credence to our interpretation of the rear part. The cubic structural plan of the seat is maintained through to the actual realisation of it. In fact now the seat assumes figurative importance. In relation to the axes of the midline of the leaning surface the plan remains symmetrical, the moderate curve of the traverse underlines this. Whilst in the two former perspectives the back uprights exhaust their function in the leaning quality, and in the equilibrium furnished by the main design, when one studies them from the side in their formal foreground function, they rise unrepentantly on high, transforming their particular figurative motive.

But stress on figurative aspects should not blind the observer; the study of this little chair is not limited to the contemplation of various two-dimensional qualities alone.

To search for meaning and intrinsic value only in the figurative aspects of the chair, ignoring the historical aspect which reflected current Glasgow architectural opinion, is to risk misinterpreting the real properties and nature of the chair, namely that it is a functional object with merits which are not any less dignified than those identified in the preceeding analysis. By reconstructing the separately analysed parts one finds again the fundamental plan which was projected as a pattern. One discovers an understanding of volume and space which rightly allows these simple furnishings to join the list of masterpieces of interior design.

In Mackintosh's work, the sequence of idea, drawing and then object, flows fluently, and therefore it is easy to find in the three-dimensional reality that information already contained in the interpretation of the graphic. For example one thinks of the solution proposed for preventing eventual fragmentation of the chair, a solution which in no way alters the equilibrium of the design. Each of the little rods placed at the joint between the front uprights, and between these and the rear uprights, represents a cross-bar (immaterial in terms of function) of which the actual rods represent the upper and lower sections.

Although he took structural exigencies into account, Mackintosh used the material presence of the points as part of the whole plan, in such a way that they are volumetrically related to the whole, in the guise of a delimiting band in a plane parallel to the tilting plane, and passing at the level of the cross-bar at the foot of the back. In the front elevation, however, this joint, or rather mark, which is scarcely perceptible in the fullness of the form which contains it, has shifted upwards. Referring to the vertical, which is the fundamental orientation of the chair, one can isolate different planes which pass, one along the back bands, one along the outline of the front tapering, and yet another along that of the back tapering. The volume of the space which is constituted by these surfaces and amplified by the slight splaying of the feet gives perfect equilibrium to the whole structure.

7/8/9
Chairs with High, Medium and Low Back, Ingram Street Tearooms (1900)

At the base of Mackintosh's ideological formation lies an approach which involves accurate attention to details, and then adoption of practical measures necessary to compose them into a solid and unified structure, and also emphasis on graining in such a way

The Descent of Night, 1893-94.

that it achieves an independent status. Such was the Victorian emphasis (an emphasis arising from a febrile preoccupation with the merits of work) which was to be seen in materials and in techniques. These are salient aspects of all Mackintosh's chairs, at least up to 1900, when his formal and symbolic patrimony was enriched with that orientalized mysticism of Jan Toorop, and those stylized and elongated figurations which arose from the research into expression common to "The Four".

Reserving for later the discussion of the participation of the architect in Art Nouveaù, one cannot abstain here from saying that no style ever conquered his personal artistic experiences and acquisitions, in other words, nothing he created shows a total break with his own most personal creative expression.

The model designed for the Ingram Street Tearooms, with a high back and a structure similar to that produced in 1897 with an oval summit, is as a chair fundamentally influenced by the ideology that reigned in the immediately preceeding years. However, at the heart of a systematic analysis attempting to determine the value of Mackintosh's furniture, is an acknowledgement of the immediacy of his expressive dynamism, whether this be seen in his embryonic productions in a vaguely fin-de-siècle style, or whether it be seen in the purity of the formal content which had already appeared in the artist's first works. It is just this latter aspect which deserved deeper study. Whilst the structure of this chair re-affirms the fundamentally harmonic scheme of the preceeding chairs, it expresses in a semantic key a singular figurative quality which is juxtaposed to the heterogeneous structure of the geometrical totality.

The chair possesses the two entities of function and form, which are respectively materialized in the upper connecting cross-bar, between the uprights, and in the little cut-outs which appear on the vertical bands. Such an innovation, along with the reduction of the height of the lower cross-bar, increases that sense of portraiture and consequently accentuates the figurative quality of the back. This new proposition has a more unified and coherent character, in the sense that the observer, liberated from preoccupation with secondary details, relates formal composition to function more easily. More precisely, in the model the artist has purified the fundamental scheme by reducing the importance of the collateral configurations. Variation from the prototype is therefore more apparent than real, since the new solution substantially respects the architect's initial approach to the treatment of space, but adds to this an achievement of extreme elegance in offering the background portrait as a pure form. As such it maintains its characteristics and its figurative merits, even in editions where the proportions are altered, as happens in the Medium Back and Low Back types.

One can, therefore, agree with Macleod that in such a work the formal dignity of the chair resides for the greater part, if not completely, in the surface figurations, and it is permissible to add that they have an autonomous existence disassociated from any underlying function.

The diversity between these chairs and between them and the chair with the oval summit is to be found not in the fundamental structure, because it is certainly the same, but in the modification of secondary details, despite the diversity of the end-product. Comparing them all, even with their common fundamental structure, these chairs all possess an individual character, the merits of which are comparable and available to analysis. It may seem wrong, therefore, to assimilate them all into the same typology. Their unity can be drawn, if from nothing else, from their relationship in function, a relationship which is in constant mutation and which replies to all the other furnishings in the interior they were designed for.

Even recourse to a rather obscure change, such as painting the chair, can produce a chair with a very different effect. The chair designed for Mackintosh's own flat in Mains Street is an example of this.

Mackintosh always managed to produce living forms. If one studies the use of paint in a chair that has the same construction as another, one finds that Mackintosh has not just transformed the object, but has created a new one. If even today, after seventy years, he is surprising in his peculiarities, what a novelty that first sign of Art Nouveau must have been, when the narrow path of tradition was so closely followed. Until then, white painted furniture had not been seen for generations. One had to go back to the reign of Louis XVI in order to encounter white furniture. In this 1900 edition, however, the characterization of the style is entrusted to the cut-outs which once more, together with the global distribution of space, state the culmination of that process of universalization of "Design" which was the most important aspect of Mackintosh's artistic personality, which was already mature at that time.

The presence of empty spaces gives the back a virtual thickness, functioning as a relief, almost like upholstery. Their composition has a latent statement which one can find in the sense of dissolving sorrow originating in the figurations of Toorop and Beardsley, and later found absorbed and elaborated in the work of "The Four".

From the opening for grasping the chair, as from the core matrix, elementary geometrical forms are born, and flow downwards. The cadence of their succession, then suspension, then appearance in the middle of the portrait, underlines an autonomous figural composition, and their division emphasizes that downward flow of wan and weeping forms. Undoubtedly, the whole composition even though it expresses a profoundly rational system, has a notably formalistic tone, and therefore, shares in that particular design characteristic which is found in all Mackintosh's works. Consider for example « The Peacock », preliminary drawing for the mural decoration of the Buchanan Street Tearooms (1896). Here one finds that the graphical representation of the plumage is all held in the rigid symmetry of a geometrical design based on formalization of line and colour.

One can give a similar interpretation to the group of cut-outs on the back, where the figuration (here without any function) emphasizes with a gently sloping and refined symbolism the downward flowing unravelling of the portrait. Quite apart from its rôle in the chair as an object, the composition of the back, analysed in its separate characteristics, expresses in itself the complexity of Mackintosh's graphic symbolism, and that aspect of it which synthesizes the simultaneous antagonism of ascending and descending forces returns constantly and significantly in his work. Besides discovering it in other chairs, its lively presence is to be noted in the Library of the Glasgow School of Art, where a cascade of central lamps corresponds to the elevation of the slender pillars. These pillars with their linear ascending continuity

Japanese Witch Hazel, Walberswick, 1915. Glasgow School of Art, Library.

are used as connecting elements in the spatial partitioning, and seem to be the sole support of the roof, and to bear all the weight of books stored above. In reality they have the static function of joining beams between the original structure of the western part of the School, the principal beams of the roof above the deposit and those of the lower roof of the Library.

The annotations we have made so far would allow us to accept that Mackintosh shared at least the reforming intentions of the Arts and Crafts Movement, and gradually evolved towards that blending of stylized flowers and human forms which characterized Scottish Art Nouveau. Here again we must underline that in the productive life of Mackintosh these phases are never spelt out as chronological phases when his artistic individuality was dominated by a particular style, but are phases valid in themselves, and never entirely forgotten by the artist who, rather, continually reframed them in that search for new forms in the figurative arts which concurrently occupied artists in other countries. In fact, alongside Art Nouveau furnishings co-existed furnishings with all the marks of local vernacular tradition. It was not surprising that the mature Mackintosh studied and developed new expressive techniques which came very close to the 1915 avant-garde position.

When one analyses the characteristic solution of certain details in a chair, one finds that what one might consider perfected versions of details belonging to previous chairs can be considered as new and individual forms, free from any previous reference.

One recalls that in the lateral figurative scheme of the preceding chairs the arc of the cross-bar is symmetrical in relation to

A group of chairs and objects exhibited in 1934.

the medial axis of the figure, and the rear pillar stretches upwards, tempering the participation with the back and with the stool of the chair. In the chair studied here, we find a most original solution from the front, a solution which the artist arrives at through a well-considered change in the line of the cross-bar. In profile, now, the typical bilateral symmetry is completely decentralized and is moved towards the front leaning surface.

The resulting effect is a tapering shelf, the maximum section belonging exclusively to the back upright. The interesting plan of these compositions can be seen in the binomial upright/horizontal; and it is a plan which releases intense dynamism in both orthogonal directions, because of the reciprocal influence of the tapering of the details.

The front pillar with the related joining rods participates only as a corollary to the composition of the totality, remaining subordinate to it in such a way as to render it free to express all its figurative responsibility.

10
Armchair with Tapering Back for the Front Hall of Windyhill (1900)

In contrast to those typical and individual constants of Mackintosh's patrimony, namely dynamic form and linear two-dimensionality as systematically recurring figurations in his furniture design, one finds here a chair which is notably singular in its figurative properties, and which can be considered, as it were, almost a Mackintosh antiform.

It is the only chair in the series where rotundity is not only contained, as happens in the already studied chairs where it is absorbed to the point of disappearance under the pressure of surface representations (as can be observed in the Argyle Street chair), but assumes a position of importance in the harmonic scheme of the composition.

This is the chair designed for the hall of Windyhill, Kilmacolm, Renfrewshire, around 1900. At this time integral planning was not a novelty and had already been proposed by Ruskin and Morris.

However, few people were able to contemplate global planning and a consequently complete materialization.

When Mackintosh was given the task by William Davidson of planning a house on a hill, he used the opportunity to produce one of the most fascinating and significant of his works.

This chair is an integral feature in the interior of the house, and one can find much to be recommended in its singular characteristics. The first component to be isolated is its barrel-shaped upwards tapering back, which is abruptly cut off at the top, and lacks the iconographic quality of the summit of other models.

The surviving sketches and drawings show it as composed of three flat axes joined in a longitudinal sense, the two laterals having a symmetrical inclination in relation to the central one, in order to form a welcoming hollow for the user.

It is difficult to say with certainty what the artist's reasons were for abandoning the original project in the construction phase, in order to give life to this curving profile which lacks a continuous solution between the two sides of the chair; perhaps because the flat surfaces, dark, smooth and broad like the back, create an insupportable play of reflected light, or perhaps because the curved profile, marrying better with the perimeter of the seat, gives a more unitary dimension to the chair. It can be said that the finished object results in something of an object as negative, even though it shares the ideological premises pertinent to the previously described objects.

When one first sees this chair one has the feeling of being in the presence of an already known and familiar form. It has something of the archetypal profile of a medieval hat about it. The back, which is simply a section of a cylinder cut in the longitudinal sense with two planes converging upwards, gives the construction a strong static feeling almost like the tower of a castle. Once more Mackintosh has recourse to a medieval ideal of austerity, strength and grandeur, here amplifying the archaic and avoiding any dynamic line.

Although he avoids formalism he has here produced a chair of extreme linearity. The quality of the lines is continually and systematically stimulating and contributes to the research into morphological relationship which was Mackintosh's particular attribute.

In this example of his work, the top or the summit, as an individually meaningful sign, has disappeared, and does not reappear except as an integral innovation emphasizing the attributes of the back. The observer is taken rather by secondary details, for example, the softly curved hole at a well-chosen position at the base of the back, and the small related brim at the top which besides having the symbolic function of protecting the user's head, has the technical function of reinforcement at the extremities of the axes.

As in the other furniture, already studied, much of the message of the object is almost exclusively entrusted to the arm/back relationship; the other components, the seat, the front pillar, the cross-rungs emphasize this message by their very subjugation.

Impressive and entirely in wood, the en-

96

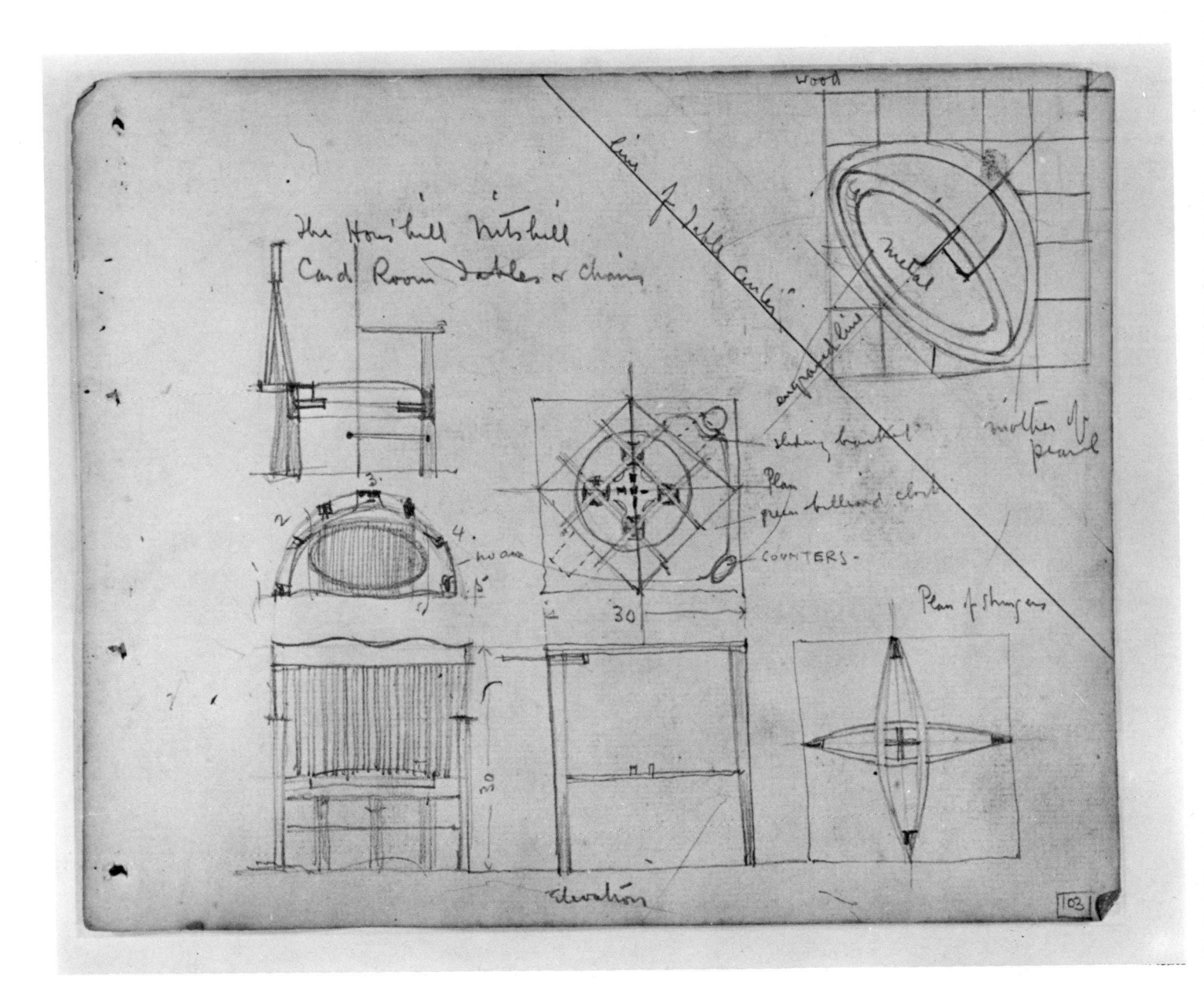

folding shield of the back is tilted slightly backwards to allow the arms to raise themselves gently forwards. It constitutes a substantial part of a hypothetical cylinder which contains the fundamental plan of the object.

The back of this abstract solid represents the remote background where the observer's attention is focused, but, owing to its protecting and limiting function, it is of very real importance in opposition to the foreground.

The medial plane where the occupant sits, is, however, the most important plane, and its importance is underlined by the widening embrace of the arms which have their largest section just in this plane, and formally express their function of encircling the user.

It is important to note Mackintosh's use of the spatial dimension here. Contrary to other models where the principal characteristic is their two-dimensional figuration, here we are confronted for the first time with a piece of furniture which has a three-dimensional conception. Amongst the most notable chairs, this is the only one which cannot be reduced to a formal two-dimensional scheme.

Apart from the dialectic relation between form and function, and the various components, the constructive characteristics already outlined and the presence of canonic forms already noted in the architectural lexicon make this model part of a healthy vernacular tradition. These characteristics are in complete contrast to the dictates of Art Nouveau, which was in full flower just at that time. This stylistic anachronism is proved on further examination. The chair is in fact conceived for a house which was itself planned in terms of the rules of vernacular architecture.

It is just in this perfect communication between object and environment, in their reciprocal communion emerging from a common creative conception that we can see the Scottish architect's capacity for synthesis and creativity. An irresistibly fascinating and rarefied intellectual abstraction is the result of Mr. Davidson's request.

This chair is, therefore, an integral part of an overall project which is sensitive to the archaic vernacular and in a sense crystallizes it, and yet it is modern in the rational distribution of space, and in the delicate treatment of wall profiles, to cite only some of the distinctive qualities of the project.

Like all the chairs with high backs, quite apart from any determined historical style, the chair we are studying, independently from its connections with the neo-Gothic, has its principal function in the decoration of an interior wall and in integrating itself with other aspects of the total environment.

Positioned at the side of the fireplace, it defines the organization of the wall, and the tapered profile of the back rises with all its formal significance to the exact height of the fireplace architrave.

15/16
Chair and Armchair painted white and upholstered in linen, Turin Exhibition and Wärndorfer Musik Salon, Vienna (1902)

In this new model very little of Mackintosh's typical elaboration as found in the previous chairs is to be seen. It brings back that aura of the vernacular, and still searches for the neo-Gothic, but only occasionally in the dimensional relationship between the back and the seat.

What characterizes the physiognomy of the chair and serves to discriminate it from

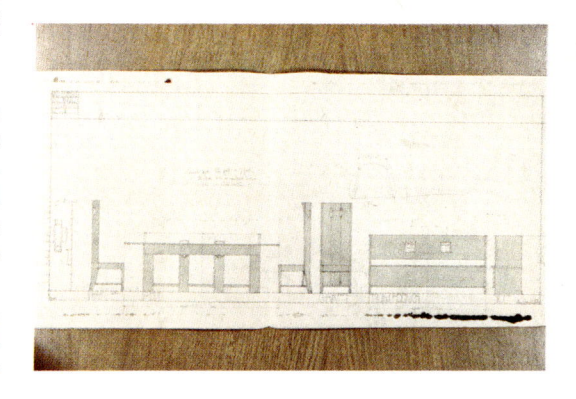

Windyhill, Kilmacolm, furniture for Entrance Hall, 1900.

Table and chair for Card Room, Hous' Hill, 1912.

the traditional is an original understanding of shapes now organized in an organically unified context, but this is secondary to the remarkable decoration to which the true message of the object is entrusted.

The rigorous linearity and containment of composition, so remarkably elaborated in orthogonal articulation and rhythm, which one has become used to now, gives way to a more spontaneous and less dogmatic creativity. Free-flowing and vibrant curves contrast the fixed geometrical lines of the preceding models and are the formal expression of the secret vital forces. Here in fact is a return to that first and original source in organic nature, the field of study of both Mackintosh and Macdonald (see for example the watercolours « Orchard » 1894, « A Pond » 1894, « The Shadow » 1895-96), and one sees that new feeling for unusual floral symbolism which was so much part of the "new style" and of their reciprocal influence.

In this first period of their marriage the furnishings produced show Margaret's influence, which was not confined only to particulars but was apparent in all his work. Thus for example in this chair, besides the floral decoration printed on the front of the back, Margaret Macdonald's presence can be seen in the free play of ornamentation which Mackintosh intentionally based on natural forms and on belief in the beauty of these forms in subjective interpretation. Mackintosh wished this chair, together with other similar pieces, to represent the style of "The Four" from Glasgow in Vienna and Turin. In any case, concerning Margaret's collaboration with her husband, some critics have said that her influence was negative. One can instead say that Mackintosh never took a real part in Art Nouveau. It would seem that although he accepted this fashion, he dominated it, exploited it, but remained far from servile imitation. He had an extremely rich system of symbols which allowed him to express himself through lines and their reciprocal relationships in logical derivation processes, and to create an indeterminate and fascinatingly mysterious impression of material things. We now understand that this rare gift was particularly Mackintosh's and permitted him to contemplate, in a unique synthesis, needs which were, by their nature, contrasting. The liberty of line and of figuration which tend to have independent existence in tapestries, carpets, materials, furnishings and metals do not entirely belong to architecture or to furnishings or to metals, because they speak of the particular problems of spatial relationships, well determined relationships, which are available for infinite mutations, and which carry in themselves the germ seed of the only legitimate decoration, that is, an integrated totality.

Such exigencies are no longer autonomous, separable in a well-completed work, but at the heart of the formation of a single and unique creation.

The volumetric structure of this remarkable chair springs directly from an interpretation and representation of a natural object. Particular care is therefore used to adopt primary plant forms for the shape of the support elements which connect them and opportunely modify them. One notices immediately the side where the meeting of the upright and of the side cross-bar outlines the floral theme, like a branch which is born at that point low down and farthest from the front where the rungs are connected, but which lives and evolves with gentle sinuosity first towards the right, and then upwards. The slight curve of the lower rear part of the upright is useful in allowing a small separation of the wall and the object and is one of these instances where the natural line blends with structure and function.

A piece of furniture thus conceived is a structured decoration and not a decorated structure, and obviously demands respect for certain relationships between structure and ornamentation. Therefore the rungs joining the uprights, which are essential for the maintenance of the chair, and would not be pertinent to the meaning of the lateral figurations, are placed inside the stool in such a way that their double track accentuates the feeling of spaciousness. The tapering of the extremity, which represents a necessary solution for the joint, adds value to the structure and produces an effect of noticeable tension.

In comparison with the chairs described previously, the back of this chair presents a notably reduced sense of vastness. Such reduction seems right in a chair which derives delicate inspiration from a flower, and it would be difficult to reconcile the solidity and austerity of the preceding chairs with the beauty of this one. The dimensions of the back determine the form of the seat, which assumes therefore this peculiar trapezoid plan. The result is not discordant, because, seen from the front, the object acquires a notable sense of depth, almost as if the distance between the front plane of the chair and the decorated back was greater than it really is.

Here Mackintosh also makes the back an element of major meaning. The formula of dynamic opposition between the upward movement of the whole, and consequently the descending movement of the lateral spaces which counterpoint it, is quite marked. An analogous process can be seen in the centre back piece which, in its upward movement, assumes the form of drapery hung from the top cross-bar.

There is no doubt that the front view is the most moving for the observer. Margaret Macdonald's decoration placed behind the head of the user as if to exalt it, is a stylized garland of tendrils and roses. Despite its subjective vitality this decoration shows a graphic discipline which is typical of the expressive work of the Macdonalds.

Mackintosh's symbol, placed almost like a summit high on the back with its harmonious and continual evolution, evokes, more than anything, the secret living energy of the plant world. It matters little whether or not it is the seed of an apple or nothing. It matters only that one perceives through the play of abstract lines and proportions the rhythms and cadences and pauses which cause deepest perturbation in the spectator. This symbol has a certain sculptural quality and perhaps indicates the apex of Mackintosh's figurative development.

Just as in primitive art the line is controlled by and, at the same time, exalts the magical forces believed in, so here the linear result represents the graphic translation of that emotional plenitude rooted in the exuberance of natural forces. This relief, which is most knowledgeably modulated in varying graduation, in the rapport of depth with height, fills the senses with pleasure to the point of oblivion.

Considering the glass inserts with their communion of form, colour and consistency as the extreme point of the long slope which proceeds almost imperceptibly from the base of the figure, as the point, therefore, of maximum depth where the feeling of the whole is condensed, the observer finds himself led, as it were, through them, without interruption, to the rear surface of the chair, almost as though his dialogue with the object would never stop.

The interior presented at Turin included an armchair and table set, which had notable characteristics in common with the chair studied above. They are white-painted pieces with noticeable iconographic overtones which establish them as more than slightly connected with the Art Nouveau period. Therefore, leaving apart the analysis of their formal merits, which are similar to those described, it is useful to turn one's attention towards those aspects isolating the really creative moments which are entirely Mackintosh's.

The fundamental structure, which is simply composed of beams and opportune mouldings, and is free from any flat surface, is essentially an organism of tensions conceived perhaps with the intention of conferring greater importance to Margaret Macdonald's decoration. Compared with Mackintosh's preceding works, which were full-bodied and figurative, the scheme of this chair is original and interesting because of its expression of lightness and neutrality. In short, the existence of the model is secondary to the design on the canvas which, because of its representativeness, is the most important element of the object and conditions all its characteristics, starting with its height, which is quite unusual in Mackintosh's works.

Chairs with such a singular structure find their most obvious position beside the table which accompanies them. Its massive construction and oval plan, in fact, functions as a stable luminous core, round which the chairs irradiate an equally vivacious luminosity with their spatial articulation.

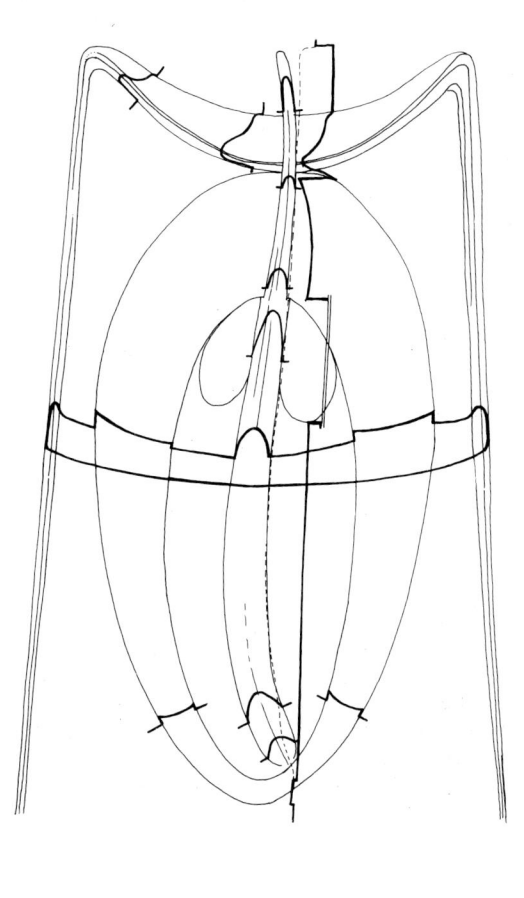

Chair for Turin Exhibition and Wärndorfer Musik Salon, Vienna, 1902, detail.

18
Chair with High Back,
Bedroom, Hill House, Helensburgh (1902)

20
Chair for Dining Room,
Willow Tearooms (1904)

21
Chair painted silver with High Back,
Room de Luxe, Willow Tearooms (1904)

22
Curved Lattice Back Chair,
Willow Tearooms (1904)

24
Chair with chequered vertical strips,
Bedroom, Hous' Hill (1904)

After a long passage of time, it becomes difficult to define the typical points which indicate a break with traditional schemes and are the beginning of new formulae in architecture. In Mackintosh's work this difficulty is more acute, because one's judgement is often clouded by the peculiarly neo-Gothic and traditional Scottish baronial aspects of his work.

Preoccupation with this more noticeable aspect of his work, may cause a more important aspect to be overlooked, namely, that his formal structure reveals an "interior space" where organization of components in an infinite series of well-chosen relationships is governed with both rigour and inventiveness and is therefore consistent with his own philosophy:

« *The artist may have a very rich psychic organization — an easy grasp and a clear eye for essentials — a great variety of aptitudes — but that which characterizes him above all else — and determines his vocation — is the exceptional development of the imaginative faculties — especially the imagination that creates — not only the imagination that represents... The artist cannot attain to mastery in his art unless he is endowed in the highest degree with the faculty of invention.* »

One can add to this, Mackintosh's comments on beauty and on taste which appear to re-introduce that complex debate of the second part of the 18th century of Burke, Hogarth and Reynolds:

« *The only true modern individual art in proportion, in form and in colour, is produced by an emotion, produced by a frank and intelligent understanding of the absolute and true requirements of a building or object — a scientific knowledge of the possibilities and beauties of material, a fearless application of emotion and knowledge, a cultured intelligence, and a mind artistic yet not too indolent to attempt the task of clothing in grace and beauty the new forms and conditions that modern development of life — social, commercial, and religious — insist upon.* »

A most definite feature in Mackintosh's composition was the rôle he attributed to the decorative piece of furniture, generally simple and linear in its harmonic scheme, but extremely complex in the relationships which go to materialize it. The relationships of movement which intervene between the diverse components of his interiors become in themselves objects in the interior. This is particularly noticeable in the chair which sometimes almost loses its function as a chair in order to become an essential part of an interior, even to the point of reflecting all its formal and structural characteristics. The meaning of a chair is therefore always to be found in terms of its overall environment.

Certainly the interpretation of the elements which constitute the object, the checking of dimensional relationships, the search to understand symbolic values, the analysis of the chair as an important unity, are always possible, and the chairs lend themselves ideally to such an analysis. However, as part of the value of the chair lies in its relationship with its environment, it must be studied as part of an interior. Only in this way can the interaction of the elements and the emblematic value of the figuration which compose it become meaningful. Consider therefore the two most important chairs in Hill House, Helensburgh — a chair with high back for bedroom and an armchair for the entrance hall. The house is built on the side of a gentle slope above the town and enjoys a splendid view of the Clyde Estuary.

The placement of the tower in the angular recess between the two principal wings, and the projection of some domestic spaces, including the bay-window with seating and the portico of the bedroom, sanctify that first relationship between the expression of volumes and the domestic fluency of the interior. This relationship is stated particularly in the most significant rooms where the correspondence between the various allocations of height and their functional use appears as one of the most singular characteristics of the Scottish architect. He differentiated an interior into two parts by indicating a horizontal plane at an idealized level. The upper part is treated with extreme simplicity in order to create a sense of indetermination overhanging the room, or even as a purely volumetric vault to the room. The lower part, however, uses rich wall decoration to complement and accompany the import of the living space and the activities which take place there.

In the sitting room in Hill House this

Room de Luxe, Willow Tearooms, 1904.

ceiling is painted in a black which exalts the spatial articulation of the lower level.

In the bedroom, the division of the various levels creates a more airy effect due to the introduction of an intermediate element. The large alcove, where the bed is, appears as an appendix to the space of the room, and its height is defined by a barrel vault ceiling. The similar height of the doors, wardrobes and windows, corresponds with the height of the walls where they meet the vault, whilst the depth of the vault is related to the height of the main ceiling. The rigorously functional distribution of specially designed objects — furniture and ornaments — contributes to the organic unity of the interior.

In the heart of this setting, amongst the other beautiful furnishings, appears the famous chair in duplicate. It is in ebonized wood with a ladder back which stands relatively high above the upholstered seat. The artist now appears to be liberated from stylistic connotations. The transfiguration of the top, the persistence of the dynamic rapport in the fundamental configuration of the back, bear witness to the absorption of traditional structural principles rather than to sterile repetition.

In contrast to the exuberance of the surrounding objects and to the delicacy of the mural decoration, the two chairs with man-height backs, placed in the position chosen for them by the designer, conduct a reciprocal dialogue as analogous heliotrophic figurations. Because of their position, they constitute a focus and polarize the entire articulation of the environment. The dark colour of the wood makes them noticeable and distinct from other figurations. Indeed despite their highly decorative characteristics, their chromatic uniformity subdues them slightly.

One of the chairs, found in the bedroom between two similar wardrobes, harmoniously illustrates the spatial relation between object and context. The other chair, situated at the side in front of the window embrasure against the light, accentuates the figuration as the fundamental element in that particular expression. This object appears to exist more for its emblematic than for its functional value, and it would also appear that the figurative connotations, necessary to the environmental composition, serve to balance its poor functionality. The sections of the uprights and of the rungs are taken to the limits of resistance, and the entire weight does not exceed 3 Kg. It would seem that in this phase Mackintosh achieved the acme of his capacity for synthesizing his vernacular patrimony in abstract terms. Complementary figurations disappear. The meaning of the chair is found in the line, which has now become both more assured and more inventive.

The Coenobitic interweaving of the top, which is continually echoed in the stairway, the lamp, the mural decoration, in the back of the hall chair, and even in the garden screen and in many other places witnessing humanistic continuity in technological progress, is none other than the old and popular "entrelac" figuration, which appears as a rational conclusion to the kinetic evolution of the pressing succession of the rungs. In the spatial context it appears as a chequered square which expresses the whole feeling of the chair. The continual and silent dialogue of dimension and shape bestow a certain aristocracy upon these chairs.

Clearly the designs used in this house have already been experimented with. Once more, however, there is definitely a movement towards ornamental abstraction, not for its decorative intent so much as in a search for the geometry of the environment. Mackintosh's worth is not to be seen only in calibration of dimensions and angles or in the play of solids and spaces which determine a feeling of a complete form, but perhaps in the topological organization of the elements in their structure and in the continuity of a figure enriched by peace and by intermittences.

The overall survey, as a method of interpretation and iconological description of an entire organized space, as opposed to the structural analysis of a single piece of furniture, is an irrefutable exigency in any research on Mackintosh. This is particularly true in the case of his buildings such as the School of Art, the Tearooms and private houses as in Helensburgh, and the no less famous Hous' Hill at Nitshill, Glasgow.

These are all works completed after 1902, and therefore after the success and experience of the Exhibitions in Vienna and Turin, and at a time when Mackintosh was most creative. These works, with an abundance of originality, mark the apex of the evolutionary arc of the master architect and perhaps constitute the most important part of his artistic patrimony. In them one can see an anticipation of certain trends which belonged to future architecture, and they were so far from contemporary trends that they had little influence even on more enlightened opinion, let alone on the average person.

The furniture, no less than the buildings, bears the mark of an intense and perhaps unrivalled capacity for the synthesis of formal and structural values, and in itself offers valid objects of study crystallizing Mackintosh's architectural ideals. In the Glasgow Museum and Art Gallery one can find the only example of the "chair with chequered vertical strips", which belonged to the interior of the bedroom (1904) for Miss Cranston in Hous' Hill. The formal theme with its fundamental verticalism reappears throughout the house, and most noticeably in the Music Room where the large circular diaphragm creates a space within a space.

The interiors of the Willow Tearooms and the Ingram Street Tearooms, which are amongst the most elaborate of Mackintosh's works, are certainly the most important examples of his ability. The first, completed in 1904, were used until the twenties when the Tearooms were absorbed into the surrounding property of Daly's Shops. (Unfortunately nothing remains of the original working drawings, but one can find some sketches of furniture and decorative friezes in the University Collection.)

From what remains of the original in the present shop, one can reconstruct an idea of the environmental organization, which is expressed in a well-equilibrated correlation of spaces on different levels. Colours and the use of fervid reliefs, which often echo the willow theme (Sauchiehall originally meant Willow Walk) and which were stylized to a rare and pure ornamental abstraction, combine to make the Willow Tearooms one of Mackintosh's most intricate works. Nothing is superfluous, everything contributes to make a unified and coherent environment. The chair for the Dining Room has an unusual design, mainly due to the lack of any of the symbolic and decorative qualities of previous works. The most remarkable aspect of the chair is the perfect succession of horizontal elements on the back in a most original alternating series of spaces and masses which, together, produce a singular and homogeneous vertical element. The impact of the volume is created in the rhythmic division of the ribs which is analogously re-proposed in the wall decoration.

Here too, the structural composition of the object does not exhaust its function in the decorative intent (a relationship already noted as important in evaluating the work of the Scottish architect), it also polarized the entire interior.

Further signs of this typical characteristic can be found in the analysis of another chair of which there is only one example. This is the chair destined for the Manager of the Tearooms. It is a curved chair in stained oak with a chequered shawl-shaped back. It creates and divides a well-defined space in the same way that the circular design in the Music Room in Hous' Hill does, and thus contributes its share to the interest of the chairs.

Among the various rooms of the Willow Tearooms, the room known as the Room de Luxe on the top floor, and reserved for ladies, illustrates Mackintosh's particular formal structure. Unfortunately none of the furniture has been recovered, not even one of the chairs which surrounded the white tables in the centre of the room. (The construction of a model of one of these has been made using photographs and some of the recoverable original sketches).

The interior design of the Willow Tearooms represents a most meaningful example of a fully cogent artistic collaboration between Margaret Macdonald and Mackintosh. This collaboration was unequivocally evident during this period, about four years after their marriage, and could be seen in their shared intentions in the descriptive aspects of their work, which were typical of Glasgow Art Nouveau where one can see reflections of that disturbing sense of the melancholy found in the Pre-Raphaelites and Ford

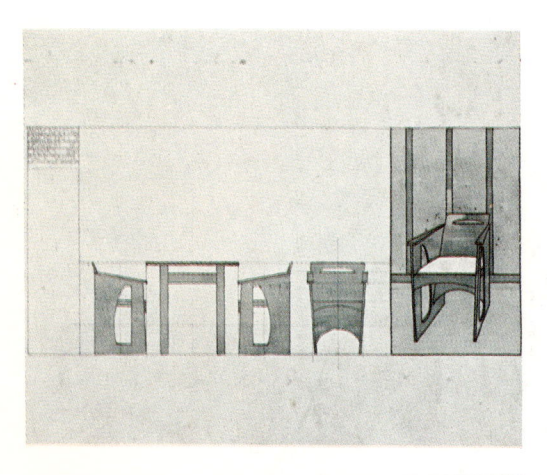

Chairs and central tables for ground floor Dining Room, Willow Tearooms, 1904.

Chairs with Low Bock, Room de Luxe, Willow Tearooms, 1904.

Madox Brown of « Take your Son, Sir », and that misty gloominess of Ossian Pre-Romantics and of Blake.

The adoption of this fashion by the Scottish artists does not explain the iconographic significance of an original artistic work. These new figurations only add to the expressive extravagance of the work. A willow panel about 1.80 metres high on the wall of the Room de Luxe, along with a plaster one, also made exclusively for this interior, are the most important examples of the direct work of Margaret Macdonald. The other innumerable figurative, decorative and structural aspects are most clearly Mackintosh's and they speak most lucidly of an organically expressive artist.

These were the years during which the Scottish artists were acclaimed in Europe. Their artistic prowess was noted in almost all cultural circles on the continent. In the work of the Secessionists, Hoffmann, Olbrich, there are more than a few signs of Mackintosh's influence. The Palais Stoclet, for example, has, on the exterior, the ornamentation already used by Mackintosh, but with a different sobriety, in the design for an Austrian or German client (1903) and also in the perimetral delimitation of the Tearooms in Sauchiehall Street.

The most interesting aspect of Mackintosh's work was his capacity to use decorative elements as structural elements which also propose a certain distribution of space within a room.

The reconstruction of the chair belonging to the Room de Luxe was made with the intention of displaying one of the key elements of an interior which has been largely lost, although the wall decoration and the warm vivacious colours of the surfaces and of the glass of the lamp and entrance door remain to witness to a most true work of art.

With its rigid plan in Art Nouveau style, the chair simultaneously concentrates the impact and the well-calibrated fusion between the formal rigour of Celtic and Renaissance derivation and the sensual licentiousness of the new mode. Thus we can consider the combination of the chequered section at the top, of the back and violet light of the glass inserts, and find an austere design with a vivacious Art Nouveau colour. One can also consider that sublime slope of the back, its almost hieratic verticalism already hinting of the Gothic, in opposition to the delicacy of the white which forms it, the exquisite colour of the glass and the softness of the material. Whilst in the front prospect the back moulds itself into symbolic drapery round the user, from the side the curves of the seat support twine sinuously like branches and, as in the chair exhibited in Vienna, crystallize that feeling of the growth force of plant or flower life.

Once more, though in a more condensed and less easily interpretable way, all the formal elements which contribute to the realization of an interior are to be found in one object. The chair, conceived by Mackintosh as the node from which the most important and meaningful elements of the formal structure of the interior environment emerge and become articulate, is of necessity the most meaningful object which unifies his entire architectonic evolution. Each chair in itself constitutes an explanatory statement.

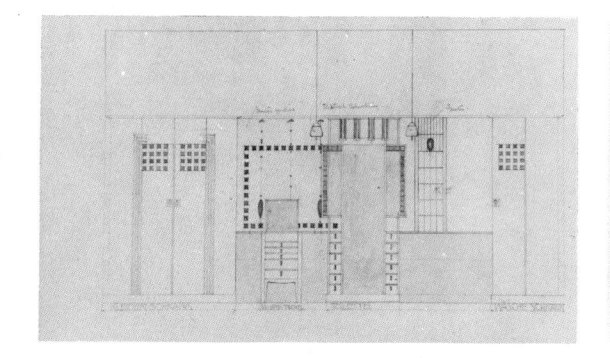

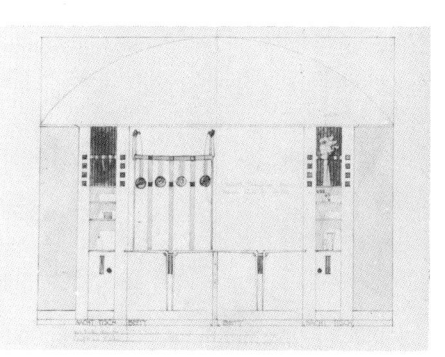

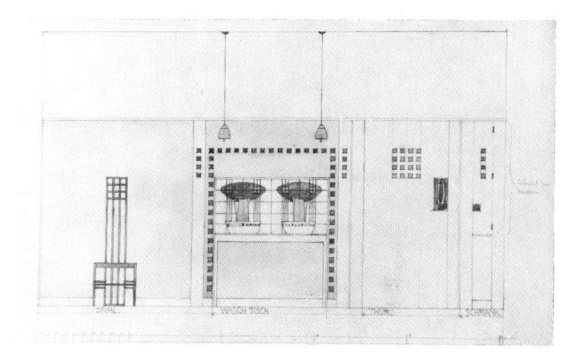

Design for a bedroom for an Austrian or German client, 1900-1903.

Acknowledgements

In presenting the objects described in this publication, my first obligation is to say that my study of C. R. Mackintosh was made possible thanks to the courtesy and the assistance of cultural circles in Glasgow. I therefore wish to thank all those who, through their contribution of knowledge and appreciation of Mackintosh's art, made my work easier.

In particular, I wish to thank Professor Andrew McLaren Young of the Fine Art Department of Glasgow University, for the praiseworthy care he has given to the University's Mackintosh Collection, protecting its drawings and objects from the ravages of time and apathy. It was he who initiated the great Mackintosh Centenary Exhibition of 1968, and he was the author of its learned and fully documented catalogue. I also wish to thank the architect Bruno del Priore, irreplaceable and expert companion in all matters pertinent to my work in Scotland; Averil Walker, née McIllwraith, and Roger Billcliffe, both of the Glasgow University Fine Art Department, for their collaboration in historical research and technical schedules relating to every object presented here.

Nor can I forget the cordiality and interest of Professor H. Jefferson Barnes, Director of the Glasgow School of Art, for welcoming me and giving me free access to all those objects in the Glasgow School of Art Mackintosh Collection which I needed for the execution of measured drawings.

Finally, may I also express my gratitude to my wife, my brother Fernando and my friend Mario Lettieri for their valid help in the researches; to the architect Luigi Falanga for his collaboration in drawings; to Master-carpenter Domenico Guida; and to Myriam Tosoni and Maresin Cavagna for editorial assistance.

The owners of the original drawings and objects here reproduced are:
University of Glasgow, Art Collection, Glasgow
Art Gallery and Museum, Glasgow
School of Art, Glasgow
Mr. and Mrs. H. Jefferson Barnes, Lochghilphead, Argyle
Miss Agnes Blackie, Helensburgh, Dunbartonshire
W. G. Blackie, Esq., Helensburgh, Dunbartonshire
James Meldrum, Esq., Glasgow
Mr. George Smith, Glasgow
Mrs. Mary N. Strurrock (née Newbery), Edinburgh.